TRIBAL POLICING

TRIBAL POLICING

Asserting Sovereignty, Seeking Justice

Eileen Luna-Firebaugh

The University of Arizona Press   Tucson

The University of Arizona Press
© 2007 The Arizona Board of Regents

LIBRARY OF CONGRESS CATALOGING-IN-PUBLICATION DATA
Luna-Firebaugh, Eileen, 1945–
   Tribal policing : asserting sovereignty, seeking justice /
Eileen Luna-Firebaugh.
      p. cm.
   Includes bibliographical references and index.
   ISBN-13: 978-0-8165-2434-1 (pbk. : alk. paper)
   ISBN-10: 0-8165-2434-3 (pbk. : alk. paper)
   1. Indian reservation police—United States—History.
2. Indian reservation police—United States—Interviews.
3. Indian reservations—Government policy—United States.
4. Indian courts—United States. 5. Indian criminals—Legal
status, laws, etc.—United States. I. Title.
E98.C87L86 2007
363.2089'97073—dc22   2006018800

Publication of this book is made possible in part by the pro-
ceeds of a permanent endowment created with the assistance
of a Challenge Grant from the National Endowment for the
Humanities, a federal agency.

Manufactured in the United States of America on acid-free,
archival-quality paper.

12 11 10 09 08 07   6 5 4 3 2 1

This book is dedicated to the many devoted Indian Country administrators, officials, and individual officers who have dedicated their lives to improving the lives of native peoples. May they, their families, and their communities have peace and know how important the work that they do is to Indian Country.

CONTENTS

FIGURES

TABLES

ACKNOWLEDGMENTS

Research studies conducted by the U.S. Department of Justice, the National Institute of Justice, the Bureau of Justice Statistics, the Community Policing Consortium, and the Program in Criminal Justice Policy and Management and the Harvard Project on American Indian Economic Development have been essential to the foundation of this book. The national tribal police research study conducted by this author from 1996 to 2004 could not have been completed without the support of the National Institute of Justice, the American Philosophical Society, the Police Foundation, and the University of Arizona.

The author wishes to thank Professor Sam Walker, who has been a colleague and co-researcher in so much of this work; Miriam Jorgensen and Stewart Wakeling, with whom much of this research was developed and coordinated; Mary Jo Tippeconnic Fox, former chair of the University of Arizona American Indian Studies Program, who lent her personal and professional support throughout the research and writing of this book; and my husband, Dennis Firebaugh, historian and educator, without whose research and editorial assistance this book, and especially chapter 2, might never have seen the light of day. This book would not have been finished without their support and assistance over the years. I also wish to acknowledge the many tribal officials, police officers, and administrators who were of great assistance in the research for this book. This project could not have been completed without their support and enthusiasm.

ABBREVIATIONS

BIA	Bureau of Indian Affairs
BIA-LES	Bureau of Indian Affairs Law Enforcement Services
BJS	Bureau of Justice Statistics
COPS	Community Oriented Policing Services
CRIT	Colorado River Indian Tribes
FBI	Federal Bureau of Investigation
FLETC	Federal Law Enforcement Training Center
FTO	field training officer
ICIN	Indian Country Intelligence Network
ICLEI	Indian Country Law Enforcement Improvements
ICRA	Indian Civil Rights Act
NTTC	National Tribal Trial College
POST	Peace Officer Standards and Training
SALETC	Southern Arizona Law Enforcement Training Center
SWCLAP	Southwest Center for Law and Policy

TRIBAL POLICING

Introduction

Tribal communities provide their citizens with police services that are uniquely their own. They employ and train tribal police officers who reflect the goals and vision of the community, who are models for their citizens, and who seek to provide the highest quality of police services available. Like their counterparts in law enforcement throughout the United States, tribal officers use the resources available to them to protect and serve Indian Country. Tribal police assert tribal sovereignty in a very real way by developing appropriate laws and rules, holding wrongdoers accountable, and asserting tribal jurisdiction over Indian land.

What does it mean to be a tribal police officer? What are the intricacies of this role? How do the tribal communities, tribal police departments, and other law enforcement agencies interact to effectively address the serious issues of violence, crime, and criminality in Indian Country? These questions and others frame the challenges facing American Indian tribal governments as they seek to advance tribal self-determination and tribal sovereignty in the United States today. The answers to these questions are crucial if crime rates in Indian Country are to be reduced and the lives of Indian peoples are to be improved. The answers depend, to a great extent, on individual tribal communities. This book has one fundamental premise: through the creation of empowered and accountable tribal police departments, tribes can seize the opportunity to advance their sovereignty and their right to self-government, as well as improve the lives of tribal members.

This book traces the history of policing in Indian Country from precolonial to modern times and looks at the need for policing in Indian Country today, taking into consideration the legal and jurisdictional constraints involved. It also examines the roles of tribal police officers, the challenges they face, and the training they receive. In addition to being responsible for vast geographic areas, they face heightened crime rates and a lack of resources that most mainstream police officers take for granted (e.g., working patrol vehicles, functioning 911 systems, access to police radios, and unlimited phone service). Tribal officers often are not state certified, nor are they eligible for state certification. Additionally, they may not be eligible for Peace Officers Standards and Training (POST) instruction.

Many tribal police departments have difficulty receiving assistance from other law enforcement agencies when they need it. Tribal police departments often do not have mutual-aid agreements with surrounding agencies, nor are tribal officers generally cross-deputized. This book addresses these issues as they relate to tribal police departments. It does not, however, address security personnel at tribal gaming facilities. Generally these security employees are employed by the gaming operation itself and are not considered part of tribal law enforcement by the tribe; therefore, I have not focused on this component here. I have also not dealt with officers of the Bureau of Indian Affairs Law Enforcement Services, as these officers are not employees of tribal governments.

Legal terms and other specific terms used in the field of American Indian Studies will be used throughout this book. A list of these terms and their general definitions are as follows:

- *American Indian* will be used throughout this book in reference to the native peoples of the North American continent. Although this term is problematic, it is the term most used by Indian people in reference to themselves and is therefore preferable to other terms of reference. For the purpose of this particular analysis, *Indian* is defined as any person of Indian blood who is a member of a federally recognized tribe.
- *Sovereignty*, for the purposes of this book, is defined as the inherent right or power of self-government. While there are limitations to this power, sovereigns, including American Indian tribal governments, have the fundamental right to make and enforce their own laws. Sovereignty can be either de jure — that right to self-government that comes from the courts — or de facto — those self-determined exercises of self-government that come from the tribe itself, and against which there is no law.[1]
- *Indian Country* is used as defined in 18 USCA 1151. Indian Country includes (1) all land within the limits of any federal Indian reservation, (2) all dependent Indian communities, and (3) all Indian allotments.
- *Jurisdiction*, for the purposes of this book, relates to the right of a sovereign, including American Indian tribal governments, to make laws related to territory, person, or subject matter.

This book examines the role of tribal policing in the assertion and expansion of tribal sovereignty, for it is through this enhancement of sovereignty that tribes will be able to fully serve their citizens. Sovereignty means the right of self-governance. The sovereign has the power to decide what laws and rules should prevail on their land. Tribal police officers and tribal police departments form an essential component of the concept of tribal sovereignty. They hold tribal citizens responsible to the tribe for their actions; they promulgate and implement rules and codes that encapsulate the concept of self-governance; and they stand for the premise that the rule of law prevails on tribal land — and that tribes have the right and responsibility to enforce their own laws.

The U.S. Civil Rights Commission Report of July 2003, entitled "A Quiet Crisis," found that per capita spending on law enforcement in American Indian communities is roughly 60 percent of the national average. This is true even though crime rates, particularly for violent crimes, are significantly higher in Indian Country than in the non-Indian community. This high rate of crime has remained stable over the past decade, with one snapshot taken by the U.S. Bureau of Justice Statistics in 1999 and yet another in December 2004. Both of these snapshots will be examined.

Another critical issue in Indian Country is an extremely high rate of suicide. Depression, poverty, alcoholism, and unemployment are rampant in Indian Country. These factors, coupled with the high number of adolescents on most reservations (exceeding 50 percent in many places), have resulted in extremely high rates of suicide, a factor that can have serious implications for law enforcement called to a crime scene.

Over the twentieth century, tribal law enforcement became the purview of the U.S. Bureau of Indian Affairs Law Enforcement Services (BIA-LES), but criminal activity continued to increase. Then, in the early 1990s the budget of BIA-LES was severely cut back, and Indian Country was negatively affected. Crime rates rose and fewer BIA-LES officers were available. This cutback came at the same time as the U.S. government articulated the government-to-government relationship that attested to tribal sovereignty and the right of the tribes to self-government.

The question of how to protect Indian communities became the challenge facing American Indian tribal governments as they sought to control violence on reservations and to advance self-determination and sovereignty. Given the high rates of crime and social problems, the tribes sought to determine appropriate and effective responses.

One significant approach to dealing with the crime rates and the widespread social anomie of the young has been the rapid development of tribal police departments. This book examines the approaches the tribes have taken to the development and implementation of these departments.

During the period 1996 to 2000, I distributed two national surveys to American Indian tribal police departments. Subsequently, I also surveyed three groups of tribal officers individually at various times and locations. In addition, from 2002 to 2004 I conducted individual and focus group interviews of custodial personnel, tribal and law enforcement administrators, training personnel, and rank-and-file tribal officers.

Approximately 170 American Indian tribes have police departments. Of these, 90 responded to one or both of the surveys. A total of 86 tribal officers from 47 tribes completed individual questionnaires, and I interviewed approximately 150 officers individually or as members of focus groups. These surveys and questionnaires serve as the basis for the data to be found throughout this book.

This research revealed that since 1995 there has been a very rapid growth in tribally funded police departments.[2] In 1995 there were 114 tribal police departments. In 2000 the Bureau of Justice Statistics reported that American Indian tribes operated 171 law enforcement agencies and employed 2,303 full-time sworn officers. About one in four tribal police agencies operated at least one jail.

Even given this rapid growth of tribal law enforcement, however, the 2003 U.S. Civil Rights Commission Report found that spending still lags. The primary question for tribal governments and tribal law enforcement is how to address the critical need for law enforcement services while also developing a format and style of policing that is appropriate for Indian Country. Developing a process for decision making, establishing policies and protocols, and recruiting and training staff are challenges that must be met if crime and criminality are to ease in Indian Country. It is these challenges that are examined in this book.

Bob Thomas, a Cherokee University of Arizona professor, said in conversation long ago, "Indians have relationships, Americans have roles." This is true in many instances, and nowhere more so than in tribal policing. In my study of American Indian tribal police, this became a truism. Tribal police administrators and personnel frequently stated that their department personnel saw themselves as the community. These tribal employees saw their job as a relationship with the tribe, an extension of the community. They were responsive to the needs of the community and felt responsible to it. In short, they saw themselves and their department in relationship to each other, not as separate entities, unlike many police in the non-Indian community who tend to view themselves in the role of hired guns whose job it is to fight crime rather than solve problems.

Each chapter in this book explores a different aspect of tribal policing. Chapter 1 examines the conditions of crime and social problems in Indian Country and presents the criminal and social issues facing tribal police. Chapter 2 looks at the historical development of tribal law enforcement, including the traditional police and military societies of the Great Plains; the Lighthorsemen of the Cherokee, Creek, and Choctaw; the reservation police established by the BIA and the military; and the Texas Rangers. Chapters 3 and 4 examine the legal and jurisdictional issues facing tribal police. Chapter 5 takes a close look at what forms of policing are most evident in Indian country, and Chapter 6 examines the training of tribal police. Chapter 7 reviews the impact of geographic distance on tribal police departments. Chapters 8 and 9 look at the role of women in tribal policing and at community complaint systems established by the tribes. Chapter 10 addresses tribal jails, and Chapter 11 reveals how tribal law enforcement functions in PL 280 states where tribal jurisdiction is concurrent with state jurisdiction. Each chapter ends with a "Reflections" section that raises thoughts and concerns to provoke individual analysis by the reader.

1 Policing in Indian Country

At its most basic level, tribal sovereignty is simply the right of an Indian nation to govern itself, to make and enforce its own laws. Self-government includes the power to control the conduct of members by tribal legislation, to administer justice, and to punish offenses that occur on tribal lands.

Police power is generally exercised pursuant to tribal constitutions and law-and-order codes. Indian nations, given this power to make laws and regulations, have both the implicit and the explicit authority to enforce them. The establishment and implementation of a tribal police department is an exemplary expression of the inherent sovereignty of Indian nations.[1] A tribal police department, if nothing else, serves as a declaration of sovereignty, of the intent of a tribal government to protect and serve its own citizens, and to render justice in a manner understandable to and supported by the community. It is this declaration of sovereignty in the service of justice that is examined here.

The Nature of Sovereignty and the Role of Tribal Police

Prior to colonization, American Indian nations were sovereign, with the independent authority to govern themselves, to make and enforce their own laws, to make war, and to negotiate peace. Much of this changed with the coming of the colonizing powers, but not all.

The colonizers implicitly and explicitly recognized tribal sovereignty through the treaty-making process. By bargaining with Indian nations, tribes were recognized as empowered to trade rights that they held over land, to engage in external relations, and to exercise control over the actions of their people in exchange for guarantees of protection, peace, and exclusivity of land use. These concepts were memorialized in treaties and thus explicitly recognized. Treaties became the backbone of United States–American Indian relations. They are fundamental to the later U.S. Supreme Court decisions that recognized the sovereignty of Indian nations, that held that Indian sovereignty predated the formation of the United States and was not granted to the Indian nations by the U.S. Constitution.

Explicit Recognition of Tribal Sovereignty by the English Crown

The French, British, Spanish, and other colonizers engaged in interactions with the native peoples of the North American continent for hundreds of years. The Proclamation of 1763 stands as an example of recognition by the English Crown of the sovereignty of American Indian nations. This proclamation centralized all relations between the Crown and the tribes. The document established that relations and treaty making with the tribes were functions of the Crown, not of the various colonies. It further established that certain lands were under the authority of the native nations and were not to be encroached upon by colonists.

After the American Revolution, the former colonies were confronted with what to do about relations with the American Indian nations with whom they shared the continent. The Articles of Confederation were developed using the example of the Iroquois Confederation, and a loose network of strong states was developed. This structure held for only a short time. The U.S. Constitution was then developed and signed and became the new structure of the government.

The U.S. Constitution is largely silent on the subject of the tribes, mentioning the Indian nations in only two places, in Article 1, Section 8, of the commerce clause, where Congress, and Congress alone, is given the authority to engage in commerce with the Indian tribes, and in Article 1, Section 2, where provision for the census counting of Indians is established. However, these clauses clearly articulate the federal nature of Indian relations and implicitly recognize Indian nations as sovereign.

After the American Revolution, the federal government followed the previous examples of the Crown, with its centralization of Indian relations and implicit and explicit recognition of tribal sovereignty. The new American government carried forth the premises of the Proclamation of 1763 when the new Congress of the United States passed the Trade and Intercourse Acts, which closely adhered to the recognition of tribal sovereignty and self-determination begun by the Crown.

Following this doctrine of the federalization of the relationships with the American Indian tribal governments, the new nation of the United States of America began to render court decisions that explicitly recognized the sovereignty and right to self-rule of tribal governments. These rulings (see below) also legally established that the sovereignty possessed by tribal governments was of a limited nature. Other rulings firmly asserted that the sovereignty and powers of self-government that American Indian tribal governments possess were not granted to the tribes by the Constitution but rather were retained powers that predated the U.S. Constitution.[2]

Over the years of the nineteenth century, the U.S. Supreme Court established a number of principles that remain the basis of the federal-tribal relationship today. These principles include the following:

- It was established that the status of Indian nations was that of domestic dependent nations with rights of limited sovereignty. Thus Indian nations cannot enter into international agreements with other countries, nor can they alienate their lands except to the federal government. They do, however, have the right to self-government over internal relations.[3]
- The federal government has plenary power over Indian matters. This means that federal treaties and statutes prevail over state law and that the federal government has final authority over the tribes.[4]
- Treaties between Indian nations and the federal government were interpreted to establish that Indian nations retained the right to self-government within the territories reserved to them, without constraint by any other entities, including state governments.[5]
- Certain canons of construction were established for the interpretation of treaties with Indian nations. These canons, or rules of sympathetic construction, provide that treaties are to be interpreted as the Indians would have understood them. Ambiguities within treaties or statutes are to be interpreted in Indians' favor. Treaties and federal Indian laws are to be interpreted liberally, and they are to favor a retained tribal self-government rather than state or federal authority.[6]
- The protection of land, guaranteed in the treaties, later came to be extended to the right to use and develop the resources of the land for the economic self-interest of Indian nations.[7]

In regard to the principle of plenary power, it is important to recognize that, while the U.S. Congress has final authority over Indian tribal governments, this power is not absolute or unconstrained. Plenary power over the tribes first arose in the case of *U.S. v. Kagama*,[8] wherein the right of the U.S. Congress to pass and enforce the Major Crimes Act was specifically acknowledged.[9] This federal authority over the tribes was then deemed plenary in the subsequent case of *Lone Wolf v. Hitchcock*.[10] However, the concept of plenary power had been raised in prior cases, including *Ex Parte Crow Dog*,[11] where it was determined that Congress could not act against Crow Dog, because it had not asserted that authority prior to taking action, implying, therefore, that had Congress so acted it would have had the authority to do so.

While limitations on sovereignty resulted, fundamental concepts of tribal sovereignty and rights of the tribes to make and enforce their own laws were recognized. These cases, and others, then became the foundation of modern tribal self-determination.

The federal government and the tribal governments have continued to define, and redefine, the concept of tribal self-determination through the past 230 years. It is a constantly evolving definition, one that changes with the political era. During the last fifty years, which is referred to in federal Indian Law as the self-determination era, there has been one overriding construct, that the tribal governments have a recognized authority to make their own laws and to enforce them against their own members, other Indians, and in some instances, non-Indians who reside or work upon tribal lands.

This authority is essentially a police power—that is, the authority that permits and enables tribal governments to control misdeeds on tribal lands. In order to control these misdeeds, tribal governments have established tribal police departments.

In many instances, tribal governments fund the activities of tribal police themselves. Additionally, tribes are generally assisted by the federal government, as are states and cities, in the development and implementation of police agencies. This federal funding may be through tribally specific funding sources such as the Indian Self-Determination and Education Assistance Act of 1975[12] and the Indian Self-Governance Act of 1994.[13] Tribal law enforcement is also supported through general law enforcement funding sources such as the COPS program. The availability of this federal funding, coupled with the Bureau of Indian Affairs Law Enforcement Services, has allowed for enhanced tribal law enforcement services.

Tribal funding of law enforcement has grown considerably since 1995, when only 114 tribes had tribally funded police departments.[14] Of the now approximately 171 reservations that have their own law enforcement departments, 164 tribal governments have received Community Oriented Policing Services (COPS) grants.[15] The COPS grants have funded more than 450 law enforcement positions within 140 tribes.[16] The rest of the tribes that received funds have used the additional funding for needed operational expenses. The remaining 340 federally recognized tribes have their law enforcement needs met by the federal Bureau of Indian Affairs Law Enforcement Services (BIA-LES) or by the states through Public Law 83-280. The Federal Bureau of Investigation operates throughout Indian Country and investigates all felonies committed by Indians that are enumerated under the Major Crimes Act.[17]

The Crisis in Indian Country

The provision for BIA-LES was reduced by more than 25 percent over the last decade of the twentieth century. Many tribes decided to fill this law enforcement vacuum by establishing tribal police services. Tribal governments have used federal funding from PL 638 and the 1994 Tribal Self-Government programs, as well as tribal sources, to expand law enforcement services.[18] While this has the immediate effect of focusing tribal attention on the reduction of crime rates, it also expands tribal sovereignty in a real and direct way.

Developing and implementing governmental structures and institutions, providing direct services to tribal members, and asserting law enforcement jurisdiction over reservation areas are efforts that expand tribal sovereignty while significantly meeting the needs of the reservation community.

Crime in Indian Country

Violence and crime are not unknown in Indian Country; in fact, they are common occurrences. A recent study by the U.S. Attorney's Office revealed a murder rate of 29 per 100,000 people in Indian Country,[19] compared with the national murder rate of 5.6 per 100,000.

The U.S. Bureau of Justice Statistics (BJS) has issued two major reports in the last decade dealing with American Indians involved in crime as either victims or offenders. The first report, "American Indians and Crime," authored by Greenfeld and Smith in 1999, was followed by a ten-year study (1992–2002) and yielded a second report, also entitled "American Indians and Crime" and authored by Stephen Perry, in December 2004. While the reports covered somewhat different statistics, both reports paint a bleak picture of the violence and crime affecting American Indians. The statistics reflect the problems facing all American Indians in the United States. Although they are not specific to Indian Country, these studies correspond well with the impressions of individuals living in tribal communities.

The 1999 study found that American Indians experience per capita rates of violence that are more than double those of the U.S. population in general. The 2004 study corroborated this earlier finding. American Indians were found to be the victims of violence at a rate of almost two and a half times that of the nation as a whole (101 violent crimes per 1,000 American Indians as compared with 41 per 1,000 for the nation). These rates remained very high even at a time when crime rates were falling in the rest of the United States.

The 1999 study established that Indian young adults between the ages of eighteen and twenty-four were the victims of violence at the highest rate of any racial group considered by age, about one violent crime for every four persons of this age. The rate of violent crime among American Indian males aged twelve or older was 153 per 1,000, compared to 60 per 1,000 for all races. The 2004 study found that the rate of violent crime for American Indian males between the ages of twelve and seventeen was 150 per 1,000, compared with 90 per 1,000 for all races. The rate for American Indians between the ages of eighteen and twenty-four was 158 per 1,000, while the rate for all races was 85 per 1,000. The starkest difference in crime rates existed for American Indians in the age range of twenty-five to thirty-four. Here the rate for American Indians was 145 per 1,000, compared with 50 per 1,000 for all races. In rural reservation areas, where the tribal police have specific jurisdiction, the rate of violent crime in 1999 was 37 per 1,000 for all races, compared to 89 per 1,000 for American Indian men.

The 1999 study found that American Indian women are the victims of crime at a rate that is nearly 50 percent higher than that reported by black males. Both studies found that rate of sexual abuse against American Indian women is the highest in the nation. In the 1999 report, 7 Indian women per 1,000 were found to be victims of rape or sexual assault — compared with 3 per 1,000 among blacks and 2 per 1,000 among whites. The 2004 report found similar statistics, with violence against American Indian women more than double that of women generally (85 per 1,000, compared with 38 per 1,000). The 1999 report found that more than 76 percent of American Indian women had a history of domestic violence as victims, and 69 percent of American Indian children reported exposure to violence.

The 1999 report found that American Indian women were more than twice as likely to report being stalked as women of other racial or ethnic backgrounds. Approximately 70 percent of restraining orders obtained by Indian women against stalkers were violated.

A predominant factor found in the 1999 BJS study was the effect of alcohol consumption. While intoxication in connection with crime is common across the United States, it is most common in Indian Country. Nationally, approximately one-third of all nonviolent crimes and approximately 40 percent of violent crimes are committed while under the influence of alcohol. However, in Indian Country the numbers are much higher. The 1999 report found that nearly half (46 percent) of all convicted American Indians in local jails had been under the influence of alcohol when they committed the offense for which they had been convicted. The proportion rose to 70 percent when only violent crimes are considered. This finding was corroborated by the 2004 report, which noted that an offender using alcohol victimized approximately 62 percent of American Indians, compared to a national average of 42 percent. This situation alone can seriously complicate the work of tribal police, for where intoxication is a factor, police work can be much more dangerous.

Yet another factor operating in Indian Country is the frequency of suicide. One study, a 1973 report entitled "Suicide, Homicide, and Alcoholism among American Indians," issued by the National Institutes of Health, set the suicide rate for American Indians at twice the national average. The rate for Indian youth on some reservations was up to six times the national average. A later study, conducted nationwide in 1987, found that the suicide rates for Indian and Alaska Native youths aged ten to twenty-four were 2.8 to 2.3 times as high as general U.S. rates for similarly aged youth. And again, fifteen years later, the 2003 U.S. Civil Rights Commission Report found that American Indian youth comprised about 75 percent of the juveniles in the federal prison system, were seventeen times more likely to die in an alcohol-related death, and were three times as likely to commit suicide as non-Indian youths. This rate of suicide, coupled with the pervasive use of alcohol, can seriously complicate the job of law enforcement, as persons with whom officers come into contact may feel that they have nothing to lose, a decision that can easily put the officer at a high level of risk.

Finally, another highly complicating factor for tribal police is the race of perpetrators of crimes. The 1999 BJS study found that at least 70 percent of the violent crime experienced by American Indians was interracial, with the perpetrator being white in 60 percent of the cases. The 2004 report corroborated these findings. This situation can be a serious problem for tribal police, who, through the operation of case law,[20] have the right to arrest only tribal members and other Indians. Non-Indian perpetrators, even if they live on the reservation or are in a personal or business relationship with an Indian, may only be detained or left to the state or federal police to be apprehended. This can cause lawlessness on a reservation that cannot be addressed by tribal police.

Characteristics of Tribal Police Departments

Law enforcement officers throughout the United States face many problems, including budget constraints, the need to recruit and train law enforcement officers, and a lack of up-to-date technology. These problems are amplified when one looks specifically at tribal police departments.

Most of Indian Country is rural, with widely dispersed populations, a lack of cell phone towers or landlines, restricted car radio service, a limited number of paved roads, and relatively few 911 emergency response systems. Recruiting and/or retaining officers may be difficult. Training can be expensive and time-consuming. The extent and impact of these problems, along with others, are addressed in detail in chapter 7, but suffice it to say that these problems create major obstacles for the provision of adequate tribal police service.

Yet another obstacle is the result of the fragmentation of jurisdiction and police service. The 1997 *Report of the Executive Committee for Indian Country Law Enforcement Improvements* (ICLEI) to the U.S. attorney general and the secretary of the interior found that tribal law enforcement was fragmented and was characterized by poor coordination and a lack of adequate resources. The report concluded that there is a public safety crisis in Indian Country. Further, this crisis is underscored when the financial resources available to Indian Country law enforcement are considered. In general, studies have found that tribal law enforcement is underfunded, with a spending level of only $83 in public safety funds per resident, compared with $104 per resident in non-Indian communities.[21] When that figure is considered in light of the crime rates prevalent in Indian Country, the concept of a public safety crisis as set forth in the ICLEI report is fully illuminated.

Reflections

When viewed through a purely pragmatic lens, the provision of adequate tribal police services can seem extremely difficult. The lack of funding and infrastructure alone would seem to condemn it to failure. This is not the case, however. Instead, tribal policing is a growing field. It is innovative and progressive, and in many ways it can serve as an example of how policing should be done. Its success is to a great extent the result of the work of many devoted tribal administrators, officials, and individual officers who have dedicated their lives to improving the lives of native people. It is also a result of the commitment of federal agencies, such as the Bureau of Indian Affairs, the Department of Justice, the Victims of Crime Office, the Violence against Women Office, the COPS Program, and the National Institute of Justice, all of which have made significant financial investments in tribal governments and law enforcement.

Many tribal governments have also made considerable investments of tribal funds in law enforcement. Some of this has been forced investment due to the serious cutbacks that have occurred in federal law enforcement services available to tribes. But much of the investment has been the result of the diversion of funds from other essential services.

This investment is directly attributable to the concern that tribal governments have for the safety of tribal citizens and law enforcement. The hope of tribal administrators is that these funds will help to curb the very high crime rates in Indian Country while also improving the lives of tribal citizens and others who reside on or visit the reservations. However, the issue of the continuation of services also arises, because much of federal funding is through grants, and when the grant period is over, those services may be discontinued. This can leave tribal citizens disappointed and discouraged.

The problem of raising the expectations of citizens is one that is faced by many jurisdictions. When raised expectations are linked with funding constraints, the result can be very demoralizing for a government and a citizenry. What tribal law enforcement programs to fund and where to obtain the funding are questions that can be answered only by the tribes themselves, and the questions require a serious examination of the situations facing the individual tribes.

2 The History of the Tribal Police

The story of law enforcement in Indian Country transcends written history. It extends back into the dawn of time, when the indigenous people of this continent sought to have order in their lives. This search for order was conducted while they were living in distinct communities and when different bands and different peoples gathered from across wide areas to hunt, to negotiate, and to celebrate. Guardians and law keepers were designated by their tribes to keep order and to protect their people. For many of these native peoples today, the modern structure of law enforcement is not all that different from traditional structures. For some, even the names of the agents of law enforcement remain the same. There have been five eras of law enforcement in Indian Country: traditional law enforcement, generally prior to 1860 (without colonial control); reservation-based law enforcement, from 1860 to 1880 (with local control by a reservation agent); federal control of Indian police, from 1880 to 1920; the federalization of Indian police, from 1920 to 1950; and self-determination, from 1960 to today.

Traditional Policing, before 1860

Originally, prior to colonization, the keeping of order was the duty of clans or specially designated societies. Often clans were responsible for the conduct of their members. In other instances, military or warrior societies were entrusted with this responsibility for the good of the whole tribe. The clan or society was responsible not only for law enforcement but also for the form that such law enforcement would take.

During early colonial times, tribal law enforcement responsibility was recognized in many treaties with the English Crown. Colonial treaties with the tribes, and later the treaties negotiated by the U.S. government, generally required that the tribes turn over non-Indian miscreants to national authorities for punishment. However, internal law enforcement issues were to be handled by the tribe itself.

The Five Civilized Tribes

The Five Civilized Tribes illuminate an early example of traditional clan-based tribal police control in the late 1700s. In 1797, for example, the Cherokees created a mounted tribal police force with authority to deal with horse theft and other property crimes. This force became known in the early 1800s as the regulating companies and later, during the 1820s, as the Lighthorsemen.[1] The jurisdiction of the Lighthorsemen was expanded to the apprehension of criminals, who were then turned over to tribal courts for trial and punishment. The crimes within the Lighthorsemen's purview extended to major crimes such as murder, rape, and robbery, as well as crimes against public order, such as intoxication.

The first law established among the Cherokee of Arkansas, prior to the Trail of Tears, concerned the appointment of a Lighthorse company "whose duty shall be to preserve peace and good order among the Cherokees in Arkansas, to suppress stealing, and punish such as may be caught in such an act."[2] The creation and empowerment of the Lighthorsemen brought about the demise of clan revenge as the model for law enforcement. In 1810 the Cherokee adopted the Law of Abrogation of Clan Revenge. This law was handwritten in English (as the Cherokee syllabary was yet to be developed by Sequoyah) and was held in the possession of the tribal chief, where it was available to any Cherokee citizen.[3]

The roles of law enforcement and clan membership overlapped in Cherokee society. Lighthorsemen were largely drawn from the Paint Clan, the clan of the sorcerers, who were said to possess special knowledge and supernatural power. Lighthorsemen often rubbed themselves with tobacco to become invisible, and traditional incantations were often used to protect and aid peace officers. Some Lighthorsemen were reported to be powerful witches. The laws of the Cherokee were seen as sacred, and magic formulas or incantations were commonly used to enforce the written law.[4]

Lakota Law Enforcers

The same pattern of traditional clan or society leadership becoming the backbone of tribal law enforcement was evident later at Pine Ridge, where traditional Lakota law enforcers (*akicitas*) became the first members of the Pine Ridge police force. Here the large numbers of akicitas who moved into law enforcement established the connection between traditional Lakota law enforcement and the federal police agencies.[5]

Akicitas had always policed Lakota society. They were appointed by the band's *wakiconze*, or camp administrator, from the membership of certain men's societies, and served terms of one year. They were empowered to police camp moves, regulate buffalo hunts, and enforce tribal laws and customs. They served as both judge and jury.[6]

Of the fifty original members of the Pine Ridge police force, at least twelve were akicitas, and a significant number were from highly traditional bands. Two early members of the Pine Ridge police force, Pumpkin Seed of the Wazaza and Standing Soldier of the Wagulhe, were head akicitas.[7]

In keeping with this overlap between traditional forces of law and order and reservation police, the first captain of the Pine Ridge police force was Man Who Carries His Sword, or George Sword, who came from a family of hereditary chiefs. Sword had previously been a *wicasa wakan* (holy man/shaman), a *pejuta wicasa* (medicine man), a *wakiconze* (camp administrator) and a *blota hunka* (war leader). It was the active involvement of men such as Sword that served to underscore the significance of the tribal police agencies and encouraged adherence to the law.[8]

Reservation Police, 1860–1880

Self-policing on a traditional level held throughout the postrevolutionary period; however, with the opening of the western frontier and the reservation period (1860–1880), the federal government moved to assert law enforcement jurisdiction over Indian Country.

The centralization of most Indian peoples on reservations and the proximity of non-Indian settlers led Indian agents in the 1860s and 1870s to organize reservation police forces, which led to the establishment of the Indian Police under the Bureau of Indian Affairs and brought the demise of clan and society-based authority. The BIA recruited, employed, and outfitted tribal members and standardized law-enforcement procedures. A bureaucratic, one-size-fits-all approach to tribal law enforcement became the norm throughout Indian Country.

The Rise of Reservation Police Forces

On many reservations, Indian people were from mixed bands or tribes, resulting in a breakdown of traditional lines of authority. In 1862, Indian agent Benjamin F. Lushbaugh unofficially established the Pawnee Indian police force. Lushbaugh selected six influential leaders from the various tribes or bands and formed them into a police agency with authority to stop certain kinds of problematic behavior.[9] Band members were used to police the members of other bands. Other agents approached the problem of lawlessness by developing a legal code of conduct that would be enforced by tribal leaders selected by the agent.[10]

The willingness of tribal members to become Indian police was undoubtedly advanced by many factors, but an important one was the decision of the federal government to hold a whole tribe accountable when some of its members violated the law. A circular letter dated June 10, 1869, expressly required that the tribes be informed that any Indian who committed murder, theft, or robbery must be delivered up by the tribe to the federal agents, or the tribal annuities for the whole tribe would be withheld.[11] Given the destitute conditions facing tribes on reservations, this could mean widespread starvation. It is no wonder, then, that responsible tribal members voluntarily agreed to become Indian police in order to help the majority of tribal members by acting against the minority who were wrongdoers.

It is unclear precisely when the federal government officially established reservation law enforcement. However, during the 1870s Indian agents for the Pawnee, Klamath, Modoc, Navajo, Apache, Blackfeet, Chippewa, and Sioux established reservation-based Indian police agencies.[12]

The Navajo Experiment

An early federal experiment in policing by Indian people on Indian reservations was conducted on the Navajo reservation in 1872. The Navajo were seen as fierce warriors who had a history of raiding Mexican and Pueblo settlements. They endured the Long Walk from their home country to Bosque Redondo in 1863. After their return to their homeland in 1870, complaints from surrounding settlements about cattle rustling and stock losses began to reemerge. A special council of Navajo leaders and the federal representatives was held at Fort Wingate in July 1872. As with the Cherokee and the Lakota, a traditional war chief, Manuelito, took the lead. Manuelito proposed that he would "regulate this thieving himself."[13] Special Indian Commissioner General O. O. Howard recruited a force of 100 young Navajos representing each of the thirteen bands and placed it under the command of Chief Manuelito. This force was charged with the responsibility of apprehending livestock thieves and was highly successful.

The original force was temporarily disbanded in September 1873 due to funding constraints and the fact that, given their high level of success, there were few further incidents of livestock theft. Navajo agent and former governor W.F.M. Hall regretted this decision as he believed that the Navajo would resume their depredations upon livestock in surrounding settlements and that he would have no means to prevent this misconduct. He then made the unilateral decision to reinstate the Navajo police and established a 200-member force in May 1874. While there was no federal funding for this force, the members were paid out of surplus annuity goods.[14]

The San Carlos Apache Police

Yet another of the earliest and most successful Indian police departments was established when John P. Clum was appointed as Indian agent on the San Carlos Agency in Arizona Territory in 1874. The San Carlos Agency was a classic example of a reservation where the traditional lines of authority had broken down. San Carlos was composed of members of various Apache bands, many of which had been in conflict with each other for generations. Thrust together on one reservation, the various bands remained at odds, causing an unsettled situation.

Two days after his arrival at the San Carlos agency, Clum appointed four leading Apaches as a police force. Their duties included arresting insubordinate Indians, interdicting alcohol on the reservation, guarding prisoners, and other duties as assigned by the agent. As the reservation population increased with the addition of additional bands, within six months the police force was increased to sixty members. This force was highly successful in pacifying the various bands of Apache now resident at San Carlos, and on October 17, 1875, all military troops were removed from San Carlos. Control over the reservation was turned over to Agent Clum and the Indian police force.[15]

The San Carlos Indian police force was generally viewed as highly effective even among non-Indian settlers of surrounding areas, including Tucson. In February 1887, under an act of the Arizona legislature, sixty San Carlos policemen were enlisted in the territorial militia under the command of Police Chief Clay Beauford and assigned to patrol duties in off-reservation areas of southeastern Arizona.[16]

While much of the credit for the efficiency of the San Carlos tribal police belongs to Agent Clum, his resignation from the agent's position in July 1887 did not affect the force adversely. Rather, the idea of Indian policing became the official policy of the federal government.

The federal government found that the use of one tribe to police another tribe was a useful tool, one that was to continue throughout the history of the Bureau of Indian Affairs Law Enforcement Services. "The Army's success in pacifying most of [the Apache] depended on enlisting warriors from one band to track and fight against those of another."[17] In fact, as Wilcomb E. Washburn has stated, "Indian police and courts were created in large measure for the purpose of controlling the Indian and breaking up tribal leadership and tribal government."[18] Thus the federal government used tribal police against their own people and other Indians to control tribal leaders and to ensure the demise of representative tribal governments.

The Texas Rangers and Their Indian Allies

The Texas Rangers illustrate another example of the use of Indians to police other Indians. Following the annexation of Texas in 1846, the Texas Rangers were commissioned to serve as the agents of law enforcement. The Rangers were responsible for dealing with all non-Indian miscreants, as well as with Indians, particularly the Comanche and Kiowa. The Comanche were largely restricted to Fort Sill in Indian Territory. The Texas Rangers were the police force for Texas and were generally responsible for keeping order in the areas of the frontier that were off-reservation.

Rations at Fort Sill were scarce and were often delayed, so the Comanche often left the reservation to hunt, sometimes with duly authorized permits to do so but sometimes without. The Comanche had a history of raiding white settlements and other Indian tribes and were feared on the frontier. As they were unwilling to remain at Fort Sill and let their people starve, they continued off-reservation hunting into Texas, their traditional hunting area, and skirmished with frontier towns and settlements, to the consternation of the Texas Rangers.

To deal with Comanche incursions into Texas, the Rangers enlisted the support of other tribes, including the Lipan Apache and the Tonkahua, who traditionally had been in conflict with the Comanche. These tribal members were used as policing forces as well as spies to help in the apprehension of the Comanche and Kiowa who had left Indian Territory.[19] On occasion, influential Comanche were commissioned to search for and bring back to Fort Sill bands of Comanche who had stolen horses and had left the reservation.[20]

The Formal Establishment of Federal Indian Police

In 1878 the Commissioner of Indian Affairs Report, section P. XLll, included the following provision and language:

Indian Police

By act of May 27, at the last session of congress, provision was made for the organization at the various agencies of a system of Indian police, the aggregate force not to exceed 50 officers and 430 privates [in 1879, this number was raised to 800 privates and 100 officers].

Too short a time has elapsed to perfect and thoroughly test the workings of this system, but the results of the . . . experiment at the thirty agencies in which it has been tried are entirely satisfactory, and commend it as an effective instrument of civilization. A simple code of rules for the guidance of the service has been prepared, and a plain, inexpensive uniform has been adopted.

An obstacle to the fullest success of the service lies in the limited remuneration for such service. The law allows using only $5 per month for privates and $8 for officers.

Federal Control of Indian Police, 1880–1920

While funding problems remained, by 1880 two-thirds of the reservations in the United States had Indian police forces,[21] and by 1890 police forces were to be found at virtually all agencies.[22] These police forces varied in size from two to forty-three.[23]

In a fundamental change from the earlier, agent-created reservation police forces, which greatly relied on the support of traditional authority within the tribes, the members of the new federal Indian police forces were generally identified as progressives rather than traditionals, and they had usually received allotments of land for themselves and their families. They were expected to set an example to their tribes by wearing modern clothing, cutting their hair, and practicing monogamy. They were to be hardworking, to refrain from the use of alcohol, and to report on members of the tribe who they believed fell below this standard.[24] This ensured a degree of civilization as perceived by the federal government and created the idea of the Indian police force as an agent of civilization.[25] It also set up an adversarial dynamic between tribal citizens and Indian police.

Once the federal government officially established the Indian police, their duties were formalized. The police were charged with the curtailment of tribal chiefs' prerogatives and the advancement of the concept of the primacy of non-Indian law as the mode of operation, a function that provoked violent opposition from traditional Indian leaders. Indian police generally served as reservation handymen and assistants to the reservation agent. They cleaned irrigation ditches, killed cattle for the meat ration, took the census, built roads, and performed other duties as assigned by the agent.[26] Some of these other, more official, duties included arresting and turning back intruders on the reservation; removing squatters' stakes; driving out cattle, horse, or timber thieves; escorting survey parties, serving as guards at ration and annuity contributions; protecting agency buildings and other property; returning truants to school; stopping bootleggers and dealing with alcohol sales and consumption on the reservation; making arrests for disorderly conduct, drunkenness, wife beating, and theft; serving as couriers; keeping agents informed of births and deaths; and notifying agents of the presence of any strangers.[27]

The centralization of Indian police within the federal government had both good and bad results. Pay was standardized and, though initially low, was raised incrementally. Uniforms were standardized and were issued to police. Horses were made available, as was feed, although supplies were often scarce and requisitions were often denied.[28] While rifles were originally issued to Indian police, this was changed in 1882, after which rifles were no longer allowed.[29] This change was due to expressed fears of arming Indians with rifles. Revolvers were then issued to police, leaving them significantly underarmed in comparison with miscreants. It was not until the late 1890s that this policy was changed.

Non-Indians welcomed the use of Indian police to pacify and civilize Indian communities. One of the most important and distressing functions of Indian police during the 1880s and 1890s was the gathering up of Indian children for relocation to Indian schools. Since Indian police also acted as truant officers, they were responsible for apprehending Indian children who had left the schools and for transporting them back to school, often against the will of the parents or the tribal leaders. However, Indian police often drew the line at using force against their communities. There are many examples of this unwillingness to act against clan and community. In 1879, when the entire Jicarilla Apache police force resigned rather than act against renegades of another clan, it was a shock felt throughout the federal government.[30]

The Dawes Act of 1887[31] and the Curtis Act of 1898[32] were intended to ensure the demise of reservations in the United States. Through allotments and the extension of state authority over Indian Country, the federal government did away with most tribal courts and law enforcement. Courts of Indian Offenses and federal law enforcement advanced the jurisdiction of the Bureau of Indian Affairs over Indian life. However, while the early years of the twentieth century saw the rapid decline of self-governance in Indian Country, it did not wholly disappear.

The Federalization of Indian Police, 1920–1950

The numbers of Indian police dropped from 900 in 1880 to 660 in 1912.[33] By 1925 this number had been reduced to 217.[34] Throughout the 1930s and 1940s the number of Indian police continued to slide, with the federal budget of 1948 allowing for only forty-five Indian police officers nationwide.[35] With the massive reduction of law enforcement services in Indian Country came widespread disorder and criminality. The stage was set for those in the federal government who wanted to abandon federal responsibility and transfer jurisdiction over Indian Country to the states. House

Concurrent Resolution 108, passed in 1953, terminated the federal relationship with many tribes. Public Law 83-280, passed in 1954, transferred full and complete criminal and civil jurisdiction (with some limited exceptions) from the federal government to the states of California, Minnesota, Nebraska, Oregon, Wisconsin, and later Alaska. Law enforcement issues in Indian Country continued unabated, for, while these states now had jurisdiction to act, they rarely did so, due to fiscal and political constraints. And the tribes in states not included under PL 83-280 continued to receive little federal law enforcement assistance.

Self-Determination, 1960 to the Present

Finally, the 1960s saw the reawakening of Indian self-determination. In 1963 more than 100 Indian police officers were added to the BIA payroll, and in 1969 the Indian Police Academy was established.[36] Through the exercise of the Indian Self-Determination and Education Assistance Act of 1975 and the Indian Self-Governance Act of 1994, tribes began to take over certain law enforcement functions from the Bureau of Indian Affairs. Tribal police departments, accountable to the tribe rather than to the federal government, were created and have expanded throughout Indian Country. The role of the Bureau of Indian Affairs Law Enforcement Services has now become one of support, rather than control.

Reflections

The complete history of tribal law enforcement has yet to be written. It is clear, however, that Indian Country has been committed to law and order since long before colonial times. Clans and specialized societies were vested with the authority to enforce good conduct. Great investments of time and resources have been devoted to the maintenance of good behavior. It is on this prehistoric and historical commitment that present-day tribal law enforcement is based.

Tribal governments are committed to the concept that tribal law enforcement is an essential and successful assertion of tribal sovereignty. While the full assertion of responsibility is a relatively recent phenomenon — occurring at a rapid pace only since the 1990s — the direction is clear. Law enforcement services, many of which incorporate traditional approaches as essential components, have begun to take the place of federal law enforcement. Tribes have begun to fully exercise their right of self-determination and take seriously again the mandate to protect and serve their citizens.

Tribal police officers who work for tribal governments have clear lines of command and clear missions. They are accountable to the tribes themselves. They incorporate the best of tribal sovereignty and self-government, and they carry forward the best of Indian tradition, the full responsibility and accountability of tribal leaders to the communities of which they are a part.

3 Legal Institutions and Structures

The role of American Indian tribal police is generally exercised in conjunction with that of tribal courts. The two go hand in hand. In order to fully understand the legal and legislative issues that operate to support or interfere with the operation of tribal police departments, it is necessary to understand the operation of tribal courts and the legal cases and legislation that frame the dialogue in Indian Country.

Indian Courts and Judges

The nucleus of the Indian judicial system revolves around three legal institutions: traditional courts, Courts of Indian Offenses (Code of Federal Regulations, or CFR, courts), and tribal courts.[1] Only a few traditional and CFR courts exist today, but they had an important role in the historical development of the Indian judicial system.

As of 2000, more than 140 tribes had their own court systems. Of these, twenty-five retained the Code of Federal Regulations and had judges appointed by the Bureau of Indian Affairs. The rest had their own tribal courts and their own laws and codes or shared intertribal courts. Some gave members a choice of appearing before either more Anglo-American–oriented courts or more traditional tribal courts. Others, such as the Navajo and Hopi, have traditional court systems that coexist with modern tribal courts.

American Indian courts have restricted criminal jurisdiction. Under federal law they may handle only certain crimes perpetrated by American Indians. The crimes over which Indian courts have jurisdiction are misdemeanors, or those crimes that are not enumerated in the Major Crimes Act. They may not handle other felony criminal cases where the federal government has asserted jurisdiction through the General or Assimilative Crimes Acts. They generally handle all civil cases.

American Indian courts handle more than 70,000 cases a year. Approximately 70 percent of these cases are criminal misdemeanors. The other 30 percent are civil cases. Tribes possess civil jurisdiction over both members and nonmembers, although not all tribes have chosen to hear cases involving nonmembers.

Traditional Courts

To fully understand the administration of tribal justice, it is necessary to understand that traditional Indian societies had different ideas about law than did Europeans. Within the Anglo-American political tradition, law is seen as a set of secular, or civil, rules. The purpose of law is to protect people's rights from the government and from each other. Justice is obtained through an adversarial system. Individual freedom is considered the greatest right in such a system, and imprisonment — that is, the denial of freedom — is considered the appropriate punishment for breaking the law.

Prior to the 1870s, Indians made and enforced their own laws. By the 1870s, however, all tribes, wherever located, had begun to lose control over their lives. The BIA, and often the military, gained economic, political, and judicial control of the reservations. Traditional tribal governments were destroyed by the removal of their authority to dispense justice.

In most traditional Indian legal systems, law was transmitted by oral tradition and custom, and the physical, social, and spiritual worlds were integrally connected. Consensus was important in reaching agreement on vital matters, including issues of tribal law and its application to particular conduct or persons. It was also important to satisfy the victims' families and to restore community harmony. Ridicule, banishment, whippings, beatings, and even capital punishment of the perpetrator by the kin of the victim were considered acceptable punishment in traditional legal systems, but imprisonment was unknown. Elders and tribal leaders participated in alternative dispute resolution, and community pressure was used to ensure harmonious community life.

Courts of Indian Offenses

In 1879, Congress appropriated money for reservation-based Indian police forces to be directed by BIA agents. Then, in 1883, the BIA created Courts of Indian Offenses, or CFR courts. Leading tribal officials were appointed as judges to mete out justice in accord with Anglo-American law. They served at the pleasure of the Indian agent, not the community. Often, regardless of the effort the judges had put into the resolution of the case, the ultimate decision in a given case rested with the agent of the BIA, who often acted arbitrarily and without explanation.

The CFR courts were charged with enforcing the Code of Federal Regulations, which was written to civilize and assimilate Indians. Under the code, certain religious dances and customary practices, as well as plural marriages, were outlawed. Shamanism, destroying the property of the dead, and failing to do farmwork became criminal acts punishable by fines, loss of rations, or imprisonment.

At their height, approximately two-thirds of all reservations had CFR courts. The traditional tribal systems of justice were suppressed. The Anglo-American–imposed system of Indian police and courts was then defunded during the termination era, and many tribes were forced to do without law enforcement.

Modern Tribal Courts

Conditions began to improve during the 1960s and 1970s when the availability of federal funds and the advent of self-determination gave tribes both the opportunity and the means to reestablish their own legal systems.

Most tribal judges are Indians and members of their tribes. Many are not attorneys but instead are trained by the National American Indian Court Judges Association or the National Indian Justice Center.

The role and status of lawyers in tribal courts varies by tribe. A few tribes have established their own bar examinations — for example, the Navajo Tribal Court. Others require lawyers to be members of the state bar. Most courts allow defendants to represent themselves, or a tribal paralegal, friend, or relative may represent them.

Tribal courts are often more informal than state or federal courts. While justice is the prime focus, tribal courts often also serve as forums for arbitration and conciliation. In this sense, many modern tribal courts have retained the essence of traditional tribal courts. In these courts the emphasis continues to be on reestablishing social harmony, not on punishment. In others, however, the emphasis may be on incarceration in either a tribal or BIA jail or on community service or the assessment of fines.

The tribal courts have strengths and weaknesses. Tribal courts are developing and implementing procedures and rules that allow them to render impartial and fair decisions. As they have improved through the efforts of a highly dedicated judiciary, their decisions have begun to be honored by federal courts, and they are being given more authority in the resolution of matters arising in Indian Country. They provide quick access to justice and reflect enlightened Anglo-American thought as well as traditional cultural patterns and expectations.

On the other hand, tribal courts can be susceptible to political influence. Given the traditional goal of avoiding confrontation, there can be a tendency toward summary justice, which can lead to the innocent being incarcerated. Many tribal laws are not comprehensive and can be badly written and ill-defined. Court personnel often are not highly qualified, there are few possible dispositions, and there can be a pervasive lack of planning.

Tribal Codes

Tribal courts apply the laws or codes that have been adopted by the tribal government. A code is a series of laws or statutes arranged by subject. Tribal governments usually adopt both criminal and civil codes. The codes in operation on many reservations look a lot like the federal code they replaced: they may be outdated, Anglo-American oriented, and poorly reflective of tribal philosophy and culture. Most tribal laws pertain only to actions committed on the reservation, although Hopi law, for example, makes it a crime to conduct religious services off-reservation for profit.

The Application of Case Law in Indian Country

It is critical to understand certain legal cases if one is to understand the law as it applies to Indian Country. For example, in regard to the right of the federal government to establish reservation police forces, *U.S. v. Clapox* explicitly approved the arrest by Indian police of a woman for immoral behavior.[2]

Other cases concern the right of the tribe itself to arrest and/or prosecute wrongdoers. The first of these cases is *Ex Parte Crow Dog*,[3] wherein Crow Dog, a former tribal police chief and a traditional on the Rosebud reservation, killed Spotted Tail, a member of a progressive faction. Crow Dog was sentenced to a traditional punishment by operation of tribal law. This did not satisfy federal authorities, and he was taken from the reservation, tried, and sentenced to hang. The case was brought to the U.S. Supreme Court, which ruled that the federal government had no authority to act on reservation lands, as no legislation or treaty had included such authority.

The U.S. Congress acted immediately, passing the Major Crimes Act, which declared that murder and other serious crimes were federal offenses, triable in federal court.[4] The case of *Kagama v. U.S.* followed, which affirmed the right of Congress to pass such legislation.[5]

In the 1977 case of *U.S. v. Antelope*,[6] the Major Crimes Act was again affirmed. In this case the Indian plaintiffs were convicted under the Major Crimes Act of felony murder, a federal criminal provision that allows a defendant to be prosecuted for first-degree murder with no proof of premeditation. The courts of the state of Idaho did not have the felony murder rule. If the perpetrators had not been Indians and the crime had not occurred on a reservation, the federal authorities would have had to prove premeditation and deliberation, which would have been much more difficult. The

Indian defendants contended that there had been racial discrimination under the Fifth Amendment of the U.S. Constitution. The court of appeals agreed and threw out the conviction.

The case then was appealed to the U.S. Supreme Court, which reversed the lower court's decision. The justices held that federal legislation related to Indian tribes is not impermissible racial classification but is instead the foundation upon which the federal-Indian relationship is based. They held that varying treatment of reservation Indians and the states within which they are located does not violate equal protection. The Supreme Court further stated that Congress has plenary authority to prescribe a criminal code for use within federal jurisdiction so long as it applies to all people within such jurisdiction.

In regard to whether a tribe has criminal jurisdiction over an individual, the first case in the series was *U.S. v. McBratney* in 1881.[7] In this case the U.S. Supreme Court ruled, under the equal-footing doctrine, that state courts have criminal jurisdiction over a crime on an Indian reservation when both the defendant and victim are non-Indian. Until 1978, however, Indian tribal governments were able to assert criminal jurisdiction over non-Indians who committed a crime against an Indian in Indian Country.

Then in 1978 the Supreme Court dealt a major blow to tribal sovereignty in regard to criminal conduct in Indian Country. Before *Oliphant v. Suquamish Indian Tribe*,[8] the courts had held that tribes possessed all aspects of their original sovereign powers unless specifically extinguished by treaty or congressional act, or specifically forbidden by the tribal constitution. In *Oliphant*, however, the Court ruled that exercising tribal criminal jurisdiction over non-Indians was inconsistent with a tribe's dependent status.

With the *Oliphant* decision, tribes lost all criminal jurisdiction over non-Indians. When a non-Indian violates the law in Indian Country, the tribe may address the transgression through such civil remedies as citations, fines, community service, and banishment or expulsion from the reservations rather than by incarceration. In some cases federal agents have been asked to prosecute nonmembers under a federal trespass law that makes it a federal crime to enter Indian lands without permission for the purpose of hunting, trapping, or fishing.

In the case of *U.S. v. Wheeler*,[9] the court held that tribal criminal jurisdiction over a tribe's own members arises out of the tribe's retained sovereignty and that therefore the Fifth Amendment provision against double jeopardy of the U.S. Constitution does not bar prosecution in both federal and tribal courts for the same acts.

Wheeler indicates that the tribal sovereignty doctrine is still alive, affirming that tribes remain a separate people with the power to regulate their internal and social relations and that the Navajo tribe has never given up the sovereign power to punish tribal offenders. Therefore, the tribal exercise of that power is the continued exercise of retained tribal sovereignty.

Wheeler and *Oliphant* together pose the question of whether tribal jurisdiction enjoys a special status. Tribes can subject their own members and other Indians to tribal justice, but they are not free to impose this on non-Indians.

In 1990, in the case of *Duro v. Reina*,[10] the court further restricted tribal criminal jurisdiction by precluding its application to nonmember Indians who commit crimes within reservation boundaries. This ruling by the Supreme Court was then expressly overturned by congressional legislation in 1991[11] as an exercise of congressional plenary power, and tribal criminal jurisdiction over tribal members and nonmember Indians was reinstated. In 2004 the U.S. Supreme Court affirmed, in *U.S. v. Lara*,[12] that Congress had the constitutional authority to overturn *Duro v. Reina* through legislation.

State jurisdiction over tribal members in Indian Country has been very limited, but *Nevada v. Hicks* recently altered this presumption.[13] In *Hicks* the U.S. Supreme Court held that a tribe had no jurisdiction to regulate the conduct of non-Indian state officers when conducting a search related to an off-reservation crime even though the search was of an Indian residence in Indian Country. The Court makes the presumption that tribal power over nonmembers does not exist unless the actions of the nonmembers amount to an intrusion on tribal sovereignty or interfere with tribal control of internal relations.

Federal Criminal Legislation

The federal government asserts jurisdiction over criminal acts in Indian Country through a series of legislative acts passed over the years for this purpose. Some of these acts are also applicable to situations other than Indian Country.

The Indian Country Crimes Act (General Crimes Act)

This Act (18 USCA sec. 1152 [1817]) extends federal laws of general application to the punishment of interracial offenses committed in Indian Country. Its present function is to provide for prosecution of crimes by non-Indians against Indians and of nonmajor crimes by Indians against non-Indians. The act enumerates three exceptions: crimes by Indians against

Indians (this has now been extended to include victimless crimes), crimes by Indians that have been punished by the tribe, and crimes over which a treaty gives exclusive jurisdiction to the tribe.

The Assimilative Crimes Act

This act (18 USCA sec. 13 [1825]) applies minor state laws to all reservations where state laws cannot be enforced. Prosecution is in federal court; there is no state judicial jurisdiction. Through it the federal government can assume jurisdiction over minor criminal offenses that have never been specifically prohibited by either federal or tribal law. The Assimilative Crimes Act, unlike the Indian Country Crimes Act, does apply to victimless crimes.

The Assimilative Crimes Act allows state and local communities to extend law enforcement policies indirectly to the reservation judicial system. However, it is limited by the fact that it can apply only to interracial crimes (it does not apply to crimes by and between two Indians on the reservation — there must be an Indian–non-Indian relationship) where no federally defined crime exists.

The Major Crimes Act

This act (23 Stat. 385 [1885]) gives the federal government jurisdiction over Indians who committed any of seven major crimes while in Indian Country. The Major Crimes Act was passed as a specific result of the previously discussed case of *Ex Parte Crow Dog*. Given the dissatisfaction with the Supreme Court decision that set Crow Dog free, the U.S. Congress responded through the use of what came to be known as plenary power. Congress immediately enacted the Major Crimes Act. The seven felonies originally enumerated in the act have now been expanded to fourteen (murder, manslaughter, kidnapping, rape, statutory rape, assault with intent to commit rape, incest, assault with intent to commit murder, assault with a dangerous weapon, assault resulting in serious bodily injury, arson, burglary, robbery, and larceny).

Indians accused of crimes enumerated in the Major Crimes Act are tried and sentenced in federal court, while those accused of lesser crimes are tried in tribal court. The tribal courts are restricted to limited punishments. The tribal courts may incarcerate a person for only up to one year and can only levy fines of less than five thousand dollars. However, the act does not restrict a tribal court from stacking charges and punishing each charge separately. This allows the tribal courts a loophole for punishing wrongdoers with more than the statutorily allowable sentence. Often tribal courts resort to civil remedies, including fines and community service, though most tribal courts observe the sentence restraints of the act; therefore, due to these limitations, most if not all serious criminal conduct is now handled in federal courts.

There are some items of particular note in the Major Crimes Act: (1) the crime must have been committed within Indian Country; (2) it applies only when the criminal offender is an Indian; (3) while members of terminated tribes are not subject to the act, tribal enrollment is not required for federal jurisdiction; and (4) the victim need not be Indian.

This legislation was tested in the previously discussed case of *U.S. v. Kagama*. The U.S. Supreme Court ruled that Congress had the power to act in what it saw as the best interest of the Indians and thus to impose this federal authority over the administration of tribal justice.

The Indian Civil Rights Act

In 1968 the U.S. Congress passed the Indian Civil Rights Act (ICRA; 82 Stat. 77). As previously noted, the tribes are not included in the Constitution of the United States. Court cases such as *Talton v. Mayes* (see chap. 1) held that tribal governments predate the Constitution and do not derive their authority therefrom. Therefore, Congress passed the ICRA and in so doing extended most of the requirements of the Bill of Rights to tribal governments and courts. In specific regard to criminal law, the ICRA affords the right of habeas corpus review, as well as the observation of due process. While the ICRA includes these — and most other rights similar to those that arise from the First, Fourth, Fifth, Sixth, Eighth, and Fourteenth Amendments — it does not include the right to a trial by jury in all civil cases or in minor criminal matters, and it does not require that a tribe provide free legal assistance to the accused.

Reflections

American Indian tribal governments are not creations of the U.S. government. Their right to act is not granted by the U.S. Constitution; instead, it flows from an inherent sovereignty that has never been extinguished. However, tribal governments are subject to legal constraints, particularly those that come from congressional acts and federal court cases. It is important to note that political eras change, and these changes affect legislation and court decisions, and Indian Country as well, primarily due to the operation of congressional plenary power.

Interestingly, however, the rise of the political concept of states' rights enhances the opportunities available to Indian Country. Law enforcement is a primary focus of the U.S. government and receives much congressional funding. Further, at this time the phrase "states and tribal governments" is often used to specify entities eligible for congressional appropriation program funding. This ability of Indian Country to fit within the recent rise of states' rights may, if utilized, become a primary method of implementing and enhancing tribal law enforcement. Thus, a movement, which has been viewed by many as conservative, may actually serve to enhance funding opportunities for tribal governments.

However, states have long been viewed as a danger to tribal interests. States have wrestled federal and tribal governments for power in Indian Country, and a body of law has developed that seeks to establish a fire wall between states and tribes. The question then becomes how appropriate it is for tribes to use a movement that might be seen as antithetical to tribes to advance tribal interests. The answer to this question will determine the direction that Indian policy takes in decades to come.

4 Indian Country Jurisdictional Issues

Jurisdictional issues in Indian Country — questions regarding which sovereign entity or law enforcement agency has the authority to act in a given situation in a specific geographical area or in regard to a specific person — are complicated in both theory and practice. Indian legal scholars have referred to this as "the jurisdictional maze."[1] It is the rare law enforcement situation in Indian Country that does not raise a jurisdictional issue. Jurisdiction is the power of a government to make and enforce its own laws, and it lies at the heart of tribal sovereignty. Jurisdiction is defined in terms of territory, personnel, and subject matter.

Much of U.S. recognition of tribal jurisdiction is founded in the myriad treaties that were promulgated, and which still exist, between the Indian nations and the U.S. government. The treaties commonly included agreements by each side to control, punish, and compensate for bad conduct. The tribes often agreed to allow the federal government to prosecute wrongdoers or, at their choice, to apprehend and punish wrongdoers pursuant to tribal law. These treaties, though interpreted, restricted, and in some instances expanded through the operation of law through the years, still frame the discussion of tribal jurisdiction in Indian Country.

Tribal territorial jurisdiction encompasses what is known as Indian Country, the land within a reservation and land outside the reservation that is owned by tribal members or by the tribe and is held in trust by the federal government. While this term was defined earlier, it is useful to review the definition Congress established in 1948. Currently, 18 USCA sec. 1151 establishes both criminal and civil jurisdiction. According to that statute, the term *Indian Country*, as used in this chapter, means (1) all land within the limits of any Indian reservation under the jurisdiction of the U.S. government, notwithstanding the issuance of any patent and including rights-of-way running through the reservation, (2) all dependent Indian communities within the borders of the United States, whether within the original or subsequently acquired territory thereof, and whether within or without the limits of a state, and (3) all Indian allotments, the Indian titles to which have not been extinguished, including rights-of-way running through the same.

Inside Indian Country, tribal law enforcement has full authority to act, subject to the exercise of federal law. Outside Indian Country, the right of tribal law enforcement to act is subject to state certification and/or the existence of mutual-aid and cross-deputization agreements. Checkerboarded land within the boundaries of a reservation can make for a complicated jurisdictional challenge. Like other areas where jurisdiction differs depending on who owns the land, tribal law enforcement authority depends on whether the land is tribal or state. Mutual-aid agreements are negotiated between agencies and serve as the basis for assistance from another agency if needed. Cross-deputization is the certification of an officer from one agency by another agency. This allows the officer to act outside of his or her own jurisdiction.

Subject matter jurisdiction defines the subjects about which a sovereign can make laws. Subject matter jurisdiction usually depends upon the answers to two questions: (1) whether the parties involved are Indians and (2) whether the events in issue took place in Indian Country.[2]

In regard to personal jurisdiction, tribal police have authority to act as to any crime perpetrated by a tribal member or another Indian. A critical issue of personal jurisdiction for tribal governments is the extent to which they may enforce their laws against non-Indians living or working on their reservation.

In general, tribal police have jurisdictional authority in the following situations:

- Crimes by Indians against Indians
  Major crimes: concurrent jurisdiction with federal authority[3]
  Other crimes: exclusive tribal authority
- Crimes by Indians against non-Indians
  Major crimes: concurrent jurisdiction with federal authority[4]
  Other crimes: concurrent jurisdiction with federal authority[5]
- Victimless crimes by Indians
  Exclusive tribal authority

In the following situations, however, jurisdiction is vested with either the federal or state authorities, not tribal police authority:

crimes by non-Indians against Indians: exclusive federal authority;
crimes by non-Indians against non-Indians: exclusive state authority;
victimless crimes by non-Indians: exclusive state authority.[6]

In general, in the absence of federal statutes limiting it, tribal criminal jurisdiction over Indians in Indian Country is complete, inherent, and exclusive. The U.S. Supreme Court recently upheld this legal position in *U.S. v.*

Lara,[7] where the court held that the tribe had the authority to bring a misdemeanor prosecution against a nonmember Indian. Lara also resolved the issue presented in *Means v. District Court of the Chinle Judicial District*,[8] where Russell Means challenged his criminal prosecution by the Navajo Nation court for domestic violence. In this case, the Navajo Nation court held that under Navajo Nation common law and under Article II of the Treaty of 1868, there was jurisdiction to act.

Tribal police are empowered to enforce tribal laws against Indians and may enforce banishment against non-Indians. Tribal police also have authority to investigate crimes committed by non-Indians and to detain non-Indians until they can be transferred to state authorities.

Tribal criminal jurisdiction is not total, however. The criminal jurisdiction of a tribe is generally confined to misdemeanor crimes committed within the geographical limits of its reservation and possibly any of its dependent Indian communities. Pursuant to the case of *Oliphant v. Suquamish*, tribes may not exercise powers that are inconsistent with their dependent status. Thus, tribal police do not generally have the authority to arrest non-Indians. Further, tribal governments may act only in those areas dictated by their tribal constitutions. Thus, if a tribe's constitution restricts criminal jurisdiction, the tribal police may not act even if acting would be allowed under federal law.

Civil jurisdiction is almost wholly within tribal jurisdiction. A tribe's regulatory enforcement authority extends to all civil actions among tribal members and other Indians. It also covers all interactions between the tribe and non-Indians in Indian Country. A tribe's regulatory authority extends to issues such as hunting and fishing,[9] water rights and water pollution,[10] zoning,[11] licensing,[12] liquor sales,[13] and gambling.[14]

The power of the tribe to enforce its civil or regulatory authority is as follows:

- Non-Indian against an Indian: If the situation arose in Indian Country, there is exclusive tribal Jurisdiction (*Williams v. Lee*, 1959). If the situation arose outside of Indian Country, there is concurrent state and tribal jurisdiction.
- Indian against Indian: If the situation arose in Indian Country, there is exclusive tribal jurisdiction.
- Indian against non-Indian: If the situation arose in Indian Country, there is concurrent tribal and state jurisdiction.

In those situations where jurisdiction is concurrent, often it is a race to the court. In other words, the court in which a case is heard will be determined by which person, the Indian or the non-Indian, is the first to file. In that case, the moving party has the choice of venue.

State criminal jurisdiction is limited in Indian Country. Generally, the power to police Indians in Indian Country rests with the tribe and the federal government.[15]

Cooperation with Other Agencies

Cross-deputization, mutual-aid agreements, and state certification of individual officers are common in mainstream policing and serve to amplify the strength and jurisdiction of individual police departments. However, this is not the case generally in Indian Country. The ninety tribes that responded to the two national surveys conducted in 1996 and 2000 were asked whether they had mutual-aid agreements with surrounding agencies, whether their officers were cross-deputized, and if either were so, with what agencies. These responses indicate that mutual-aid agreements are more common than is cross-deputization of officers.

The 2000 national survey of tribal law enforcement agencies reflected that only forty-three of seventy-six tribal law enforcement agencies had established mutual-aid agreements with surrounding jurisdictions or had had their officers cross-deputized. Only ten of the seventy-six tribal police officers surveyed individually in fall 2003 reported that they were state certified.

Cross-Deputization

Issues arise where state and tribal lands meet. The relationship between state and local police and tribal police is one that is complicated by many factors, as jurisdiction to act is something that is fiercely protected by law enforcement. Cross-deputization of law enforcement personnel is one solution to the problems that exist where state and tribal lands are contiguous and intermingled.

Under this procedure, tribal police are given deputy status by state authorities, and state or local police are given deputy status by tribal officials. With this, both the tribal police and state law enforcement have the power to arrest wrongdoers, whether or not Indian and whether or not on the reservation.

Cross-deputization allows officers to call for assistance from officers of surrounding jurisdictions. This can be a benefit for an officer who is in need of a cover officer in an outlying area, which might be closer to another jurisdiction than to assistance from his or her own. For many tribes, however, the fact that the cross-deputization of state or local officers also allows these officers to act on reservation lands is not acceptable. Furthermore, there are strings attached to having tribal officers cross-deputized. Tribal police are often trained differently by the tribe than state or local police. Generally, tribal officers are not state certified. Thus, many state and local agencies do not recognize their training as adequate and will not cooperate with them in a collegial manner on-site at an incident.

Although cross-deputization may seem like a good idea, it can be fairly rare between state and tribal jurisdictions. State certification is typically required for a tribal officer to act off-reservation. State certification requires that an officer receive training in a state-authorized law enforcement academy. This is often a problem in Indian Country, where funding for off-site training, particularly for a long period of time, may be unavailable. Also, individual officers may not be eligible for state certification due to educational standards or other issues, including criminal or personal background or physical competency. Another stumbling block is that sometimes only one agency wants to cross-deputize, which, given the requirement of reciprocity, can preclude cross-deputization of officers or mutual-aid agreements between law enforcement jurisdictions.

The data related to cross-deputization of tribal law enforcement indicated that it is relatively rare for tribal police officers to be cross-deputized. Forty-three (48 percent) of the ninety tribes in the national sample who responded to this question had at least one officer who was cross-deputized with at least one other agency. However, given the number of officers employed, relatively few were actually cross-deputized.[16] Approximately eight tribes (9 percent) reported that their officers were cross-deputized with other tribal police departments, seven (8 percent) with city police, thirty-one (34 percent) with county sheriffs, and nine (10 percent) with state police.

Given the problems with high crime rates and the challenges tribal law enforcement faces in providing services (particularly with respect to low staffing levels, high attrition, and the impact of the great distances patrolled on most reservations), this inability to call on nearby jurisdictions for assistance can be devastating.

Mutual-Aid Agreements

Mutual-aid agreements with surrounding state and local jurisdictions allow tribal police departments to obtain assistance from these agencies for officers who need assistance in an outlying area, or for tribal police departments to receive law enforcement assistance in case of an emergency.

Mutual aid, however, is a negotiated contract and requires reciprocity. Further, officers brought in from another agency are generally under the command of their own departments and police according to their own protocols and procedures, something that can be a problem for tribes, whose protocols and procedures can be very different from those of mainstream police departments.

The nationwide sample indicated that fifty-seven tribal police departments (63 percent) had mutual-aid agreements with at least one other jurisdiction. Of the nationwide total, nineteen tribes (21 percent) had existing mutual-aid agreements with other tribal police departments, thirty (33 percent) with city police, fifty-two (58 percent) with county sheriff's departments, and nineteen (21 percent) with state police.

Issues for Cross-Deputization and Mutual-Aid Agreements

The tribes were queried about problems with other agencies regarding cross-deputization and mutual aid. Sixteen tribes in the national sample responded to this question. While this number is small, the responding tribes were a representative sample.

The experiences of the sixteen tribes were similar. Most of the tribes cited problems with the county sheriff that centered on a lack of trust. A number stated that their agreements were unwritten and that they had difficulty holding the county sheriffs to the agreements. Two respondents specifically cited problems with the tribal council. Thus one can attribute the infrequency of cross-deputization agreements to the suspicion and lack of trust that reportedly prevails between tribal police and surrounding law enforcement agencies, with the most prevalent problems occurring with county governments and county sheriffs.

Fresh Pursuit

Under common law, officers may pursue a felon from one jurisdiction to another if they are in fresh pursuit of a suspect. The problems faced when this flight occurs in any criminal justice situation are complicated enough, but when the state and Indian Country are involved, they are even more so. With most state jurisdictions there generally are agreements in place, but this is not always the case when the adjoining jurisdiction is Indian. Another complication is that many Indian tribes do not want state officials to be able to pursue Indian suspects onto reservations unless the state official is cross-deputized and the Indian has violated a federal or tribal law.

Implied Consent

Jurisdiction over offenses committed by non-Indians in Indian Country is a very difficult issue. Some tribes have adopted implied consent ordinances that are patterned after motor vehicle laws. These ordinances state that any person who comes onto the reservation consents, by virtue of his or her entry onto the reservation, to the jurisdiction of the tribal police and courts.

While both the U.S. secretary of the interior and the solicitor general have taken the position that these ordinances are invalid, they have not been done away with. In the *Oliphant* decision the Supreme Court refused to uphold such a statute, but it was not argued on an implied consent basis. It is, therefore, unclear whether such ordinances should be struck down.

Extradition

Extradition is the surrender of a prisoner by one sovereign (the asylum state) to another sovereign (the demanding state) so that the criminal or fugitive may be dealt with according to the laws of the demanding state. This idea bothers many tribes because the Indian justice system differs significantly from the federal system.

Extradition has never been popular with Indians. Historically, for example, many southern Indian tribal lands were sanctuaries for escaping slaves and indentured servants. Thus, extradition became a problem even in early treaties. In *Merrill v. Turtle*,[17] the Supreme Court held that the state has no power to arrest Indians in Indian Country for crimes committed elsewhere. As long as a tribe enacted some type of extradition ordinance, thus evidencing an exercise of self-government, states could not intrude into this area unless authorized to do so by Congress. However, the recent case of *Nevada v. Hicks* has changed this somewhat.[18] Here the Supreme Court held that the tribe had no jurisdiction to regulate state officers for their conduct in conducting a search arising from an alleged off-reservation crime in an Indian residence on trust land so long as no essential rights of tribal self-government were at issue.

Reflections

Jurisdiction can be a complicated issue involving the intersection of geography and responsibility. The challenges of working with and in Indian Country can be formidable. However, when there are clear rules and regulations, practical rules of thumb, and an openness to resolving problems and issues, jurisdiction can be sorted out. Tribal police are generally highly cooperative and easy to work with. They welcome collaboration and the respect of other law enforcement agencies. Where criminal jurisdiction is at issue, the entity that has jurisdiction in a given situation can depend on many factors, and many factors can affect the decision. The best approach is to work things out in collaboration. It is important to remember the bright line rule, that the state does not have jurisdiction where essential rights of tribal self-government or the right to control internal relations are at issue.[19]

5 Tribal Policing Models

For much of the twentieth century, policing in the non-Indian community followed the professional model.[1] This model's emphasis on technology, specialized police activities, and the restricted use of police discretion does not conform to the concept of peacekeeping, the style of policing most commonly used in traditional or rural communities. Recently, however, a community-policing model has begun to take hold. This model places its emphasis on crime prevention and enlists the community for support and problem solving, making it a natural fit in Indian Country.

Professional-style policing in the United States is rooted in the Anglo-American concepts of law and government that were brought to this country by the first English settlers. In brief, this legal tradition is individualistic, placing a high value on the rights of the individual vis-à-vis government. In this respect, it is different from the legal traditions that prevail in continental Europe, which give far greater weight to the powers of the state. The individualistic ethos is also quite different from the more communal and collective traditions of the American Indian community.[2]

With respect to law enforcement institutions, the Anglo-American tradition emphasizes a strict separation between government officials and citizens. The rights of the latter enjoy the highest priority, and government officials are entitled to use only those powers that are expressly granted to them. Moreover, these powers are strictly limited by the Bill of Rights, with statutes and court decisions interpreting and amplifying its various provisions. Anglo-American legal culture has become even more rights oriented in the last three decades (as in, for example, the development of such notions as a right to privacy and the rights of specific groups such as prisoners, students, and the poor).[3]

Law enforcement professionalism, as it has developed in the twentieth century, has emphasized the impersonality inherent in the Anglo-American legal tradition.[4] That is to say, the individual police officer, in dealing with an individual citizen, is expected to suppress all personal feelings about the citizen and his or her actions. The officer is expected to enforce the law with cold and impersonal efficiency. Or, in the language of the cops themselves, the officer is expected to go by the book. This impersonality represents an attempt to ensure equal justice, one of the highest values of Anglo-American law, and to suppress personal factors that might represent bias against a particular group.

Finally, law enforcement professionalism has been pursued through bureaucratization, with police services delivered through large and complex organizations operating on the basis of written and impersonal rules.[5] In short, the essential nature of American law enforcement, from basic legal principles to police organizational structures, is very much in conflict with the communal and informal aspects of American Indian culture.

The opposite of this professional approach to police services is the concept of community policing, an approach that is beginning to take hold in the non-Indian community. The community policing approach is widespread within Indian Country and is the model for most tribal police departments. Community policing has, at its heart, the belief that controlling violence and criminality is best achieved with the full cooperation and assistance of the community. This approach to policing emphasizes the concepts of restorative justice and the enhancement of community cohesion and action, ideas that fit well within Indian Country and with many women police officers.

The community policing approach of proactive peacekeeping rather than arrests and crime control after an incident fits tribal law enforcement well, as does an emphasis on the responsibility and accountability of law enforcement to the community rather than only to the department's chain of command.[6] The devolution of power to and community consultation with a broad-based circle of responsible leaders is a common approach to decision making regarding many issues in Indian communities. This element alone could greatly enhance the work of police in Indian communities.

Cultural Conflict

The interaction between law enforcement and American Indians has entailed one of the most challenging sets of negotiations facing Indian Country and its peoples since colonization.[7] Law enforcement, in the way it is commonly conducted in the United States, is a foreign concept to most American Indian communities. The concept of professionalized policing, with its emphasis on technology, specialized police activities, and restricted use of police discretion, does not conform with the style of peacekeeping most commonly used in traditional or rural communities.

The Western style of law enforcement was imposed on Indian peoples by the U.S. government through the use of the Plenary Power Doctrine. The

U.S. Supreme Court created this doctrine in the early 1800s, specifically in *Kagama v. U.S.*,[8] and later fully delineated it in *Lone Wolf v. Hitchcock*.[9] The concept of plenary power maintains that the U.S. government has absolute power over Indian tribes and peoples irrespective of tribal sovereignty, treaty rights, or even covenants of international human rights. External law enforcement, relying as it does on the control of behavior by outside forces rather than by self-discipline or the action of family, clan, or tribe, does not fit Indian traditions.

Given the overlay of the imposed structure on the traditional systems, the relationship between Indian peoples and law enforcement officials, even Indian police, has been difficult. The example of the 1890 killing of Sitting Bull, one of the greatest medicine men of the Great Sioux Nation, by Indian police employees of the U.S. government is one of the examples still given when Indian peoples discuss law enforcement on reservations. This killing, which occurred after Sitting Bull had voluntarily turned himself in for embracing the Ghost Dance religion, is often cited as evidence to support Indian contentions that police, and the policing of Indian communities, are suspect and not in the best interest of Indian peoples. Unfortunately, this is not the only example of the bad policing of Indian communities.

Problems with Professionalized Policing in Indian Country

The concept of professionalization dominates policing in the United States. The development of standardized codes and protocols, and the standardization of training and structures of administration, are widely perceived as worthy goals. However, as in the inner cities of the United States, there are many problems with a professionalized policing approach as it is attempted in Indian Country. Professionalized policing is based on an adversarial system, with the police officers holding the thin blue line against wrongdoers for the benefit of an uninvolved community. It is based on quick response to calls for service and on a hierarchical system of management and decision making. This structure and these emphases, by their nature, are difficult to apply in Indian Country.[10]

Much of Indian Country is rural. The populations can be widely dispersed, often reached by unpaved and unmarked roads. According to the national survey of American Indian tribal police, most tribal police agencies have ten or fewer sworn officers, and only half have 911 emergency response systems.[11] Thus a conventional service response approach to policing can be remarkably ineffective.

The situation facing American Indian tribal police is particularly difficult. As stated previously, the 1997 *Report of the Executive Committee for Indian Country Law Enforcement Improvements* found that there was fragmentation, poor coordination, and a lack of adequate resources in tribal law enforcement. In addition to the jurisdictional coordination problems discussed previously, there are networks of reciprocity and responsibility within Indian communities that can unite when faced with the imposition of a law about which they may know little and which they may not support. Couple these factors with a historical distrust of police, be they Indian or non-Indian, and a situation is created that may not be best policed with conventional methods.

The Relationship between Tribal Sovereignty and Community Empowerment

However difficult the establishment and implementation of tribal law enforcement agencies may be in Indian Country, the benefits that may accrue to tribal communities are significant. In recent years, American Indian tribal sovereignty has been under attack by Congress and the U.S. Supreme Court. Court decisions such as that of *Seminole Tribe of Florida v. Florida* have been setbacks for the assertion of tribal rights to self-determination.[12] Legislation such as that proposed in the 106th Congress by Slade Gorton (R-Washington), which attempts to restrict tribal sovereignty, threatens tribal governments and frustrates the movement toward tribal community empowerment.[13]

The development and promulgation of a strategy to further tribal sovereignty, self-determination, and community empowerment in this hostile environment are critical if Indian Country is to survive and prosper. However, the question arises as to how this strategy can best develop. One way that is being advanced is the pursuit of de facto sovereignty, that sovereignty which arises naturally from the undertaking of the competent provision of essential government services whether or not it is explicitly permitted under existing state or federal laws. Although de jure tribal sovereignty, manifesting from legislation and court decisions, is under attack, the concept of de facto sovereignty is on the rise and is supported by the effort of tribal governments to provide law enforcement services to their members. One of the primary ways in which a tribal government can assert de facto sovereignty is through the provision of essential services — including law enforcement services — to their members.

An expression of this sovereignty can be found in the style and structure of law enforcement chosen by a tribe. A broad variety of effective law enforcement institutions is available. Each tribe's challenge is to decide what form best fits the needs of their specific tribal community.

Varieties of Indian Law Enforcement

My national study conducted in 2000 revealed that approximately 170 reservations had law enforcement departments at that time. This number reflects a period of significant growth during the 1990s. Tribal policing is a growth industry, with the number of tribal police departments expanding year by year. The funding and form of tribal policing are also in flux. The growth continues, however, and we need to take a careful look at how the departments are being planned and implemented and what approaches tribes are taking to the development of appropriate protocols and procedures.

Tribal Law Enforcement Structures

The 2000 study found that five forms of law enforcement agencies are operating within Indian Country. These forms are not mutually exclusive, and different components often act simultaneously within the boundaries of a given reservation. Given this, there can be confusion when jurisdictions cross or when different agencies have dual responsibility on Indian lands.

The five agencies that have jurisdiction over Indian Country in various situations are the Bureau of Indian Affairs Law Enforcement Services (BIA-LES); police officers funded through the Indian Self-Determination and Education Assistance Act (PL 93-638); police officers funded through the Indian Self-Determination Act of 1994 (PL 103-413); tribally funded officers; and state law enforcement agencies pursuant to PL 280.[14] Table 5.1

Table 5.1   Types of Indian Police Departments and Their Characteristics, 1995

	Public Law 93-638	BIA	Self-governance	Tribally funded	Public Law 83-280
Number	88	64	22	4	—
Trend	Increasing	Reducing	None	None	None
Administering entity	Tribe	U.S. government (BIA)	Tribe	Tribe	State or local law enforcement agencies
Entity employing officers	Tribe	U.S. government	Tribe	Tribe	State or local law enforcement agencies
Funding	Federal (often with tribal contribution)	U.S. government	Tribe	Tribe	Primarily state and/or local entities

sets forth the different types of policing in Indian Country. It was developed from a 1995 study; thus the numbers differ from the national study conducted from 1996 to 2000.[15]

Two of the types of agencies involve the Bureau of Indian Affairs (BIA-LES and PL 93-638). Traditionally, the BIA had responsibility for all law enforcement on Indian reservations; the states had none. This changed with the 1953 passage of Public Law 280.[16] For a number of years, the exercise of federal plenary power meant that few if any Indian nations in PL 280 states developed police departments. Now, however, throughout the United States, even where PL 280 applies, many Indian nations have their own tribal police that they fund and control. Tribal police departments often operate on reservations covered by other forms of law enforcement, including law enforcement programs funded through the BIA, PL 93-638, and/or self-governance. All of this, of course, results in problems of overlapping jurisdiction and conflicts of law.

The Bureau of Indian Affairs Law Enforcement Services (BIA-LES)

On sixty-four reservations in 2000 the police were BIA-LES personnel funded and directed by the bureau, with little or no accountability to the tribal councils or tribal governments resident on a given reservation. Regardless of policies or ordinances adopted by the tribal government (for example, domestic violence protocols or mandatory arrest policies), bureau policies are controlling, and any concerns regarding law enforcement conduct or procedures must be addressed through the regional or national BIA administration.

Public Law 93-638

By 2000, approximately ninety tribes had exercised their rights under PL 93-638 and had taken over law enforcement functions, in whole or in part, from the BIA. Through this act, the tribe must enter into an agreement with the bureau and sign a contract mandating certain law enforcement activities. The tribe agrees to provide those mandated services in exchange for federal funding through the BIA. There is no control mechanism, however, to ensure that the services are in fact provided, nor are there any external standards against which the services provided are routinely measured. However, police departments contracted through PL 93-638 are directly accountable to the tribe and have codes and ordinances that reflect the tribal needs and situation.

Tribally Funded Police

An ever-growing number of reservations (in 2000 approximately sixty) have tribally funded police. These departments are directly controlled and accountable to the tribal governments. The reservations are free to conduct their law enforcement activities as they see fit, which has resulted in significantly different training and qualifications for personnel. The codes, policies, and police protocols, where they are in place, vary widely.

Self-Governance

As of 2000, twenty-five tribes were directing their own law enforcement activities under the Indian Self-Determination Act of 1994 (PL 103-413). This act empowers the secretary of the interior, upon the request of a tribe, to grant funds for the purpose of strengthening or improving tribal government, including the provision of law enforcement services, the nature of which is determined by the tribe. Although a reporting requirement exists within the act, the nature and contents of the report are not delineated. The provision of tribal law enforcement services through HR 4842 allows for police services that are fully accountable to the tribe and that reflect tribal needs and vision.

State Law Enforcement Pursuant to Public Law 280

Thirty-nine reservations and 106 rancherias (small, rural Indian areas, many of which are not federally recognized) are situated within those states having law enforcement authority pursuant to PL 280.[17] The BIA has no authority to act in these areas. Often, whether due to the relatively remote locations of the Indian areas or to negligence or unwillingness, the local sheriff does not provide adequate law enforcement services to the rancherias. This has forced a number of tribes to try to fend for themselves or to do without.[18]

Resources and Staffing Problems

The challenge of providing adequate law enforcement services is a significant one for American Indian tribal police departments. Budgetary constraints, a shortage of personnel, and large rural jurisdictions create problems, and the commitment to tribal sovereignty can negatively affect the willingness of the tribal government to enter into cooperative agreements with non-Indian police agencies.

Personnel

The 1996 national study revealed that more than half (54.8 percent) of those that responded to the survey had ten or fewer sworn officers, and only 13 percent had twenty-one or more (see fig. 5.1). The relatively small size of most of these departments is comparable to most police departments in rural areas throughout the United States. It is difficult for small tribal police departments to have specialized units. Instead, the officers are generalists who are required to meet the needs of tribal members across a sometimes wide geographic area.

Almost half of all tribal police agencies (46.6 percent) have operating budgets of $500,000 or less. Most agencies (41.4 percent) report that the BIA provides all of their operating budget. Only 17.2 percent indicate that they receive none of their budget from the BIA. The fact that a large proportion of tribes receive all or a significant level of law enforcement services from the BIA raises the issue of accountability. The BIA is not answerable to the tribes for which it provides services. Whereas law enforcement services are critical and the manner in which they are provided can be a major point

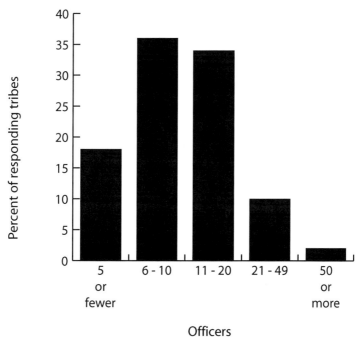

Figure 5.1. Sworn officers per responding tribal police department in 1996.

of community contention, the fact that an unaccountable agency provides these services can be extremely problematic.

Half of the responding agencies (thirty-one) provided usable data on reservation populations, which permitted the calculation of police:population ratios. Extreme variations exist in these ratios.

The *Report of the Executive Committee for Indian Country Law Enforcement Improvements* (ICLEI) found a chronic shortage of personnel in tribal law enforcement agencies.[19] The *Uniform Crime Report for Indian Country* found that it had a police:community ratio of 1.3 officers per 1,000 population.[20] Non-Indian communities of less than 10,000 people have a police:population ratio of 2.9 officers per 1,000 citizens. The Bureau of Justice Statistics census for 1996 found a ratio of between 1.8 and 2.0 per 1,000 residents in rural states. Thus, in both the national surveys the ratio of Indian law enforcement officers to community residents is far less than for comparable non-Indian police agencies.[21]

The ICLEI report stated, for example, that the Navajo Nation, with its 17.5 million acres, had an officer-to-citizen ratio of only 0.9 per 1,000. It estimated that the overall police:population ratio was half of the equivalent ratio for non-Indian communities. According to the 1996 national study, about two-thirds of all reservations have police:population ratios that are either higher or much higher than equivalent non-Indian communities.

The national study found that approximately a third of the reservations that responded to this question (eleven out of thirty-one) have police:population ratios in the range of 1 to 3 per 1,000, a ratio that is roughly comparable to most cities and counties in the United States. About one-fourth (eight out of thirty-one) have relatively high ratios (3 to 10 per 1,000). Another third, however, have extremely high police:population ratios. Seven reservations have ratios in the range of 11 to 25 per 1,000, while four have ratios in excess of 25 per 1,000. One tribe reported a police:population ratio of 140 per 1,000, and another reported a ratio of 240 per 1,000. Only one tribe reported a ratio of less than 1 per 1,000.

Given these ratios, it is hard to explain the findings of the ICLEI report. Perhaps part of the explanation is that the report was based on aggregate data, not on data from individual tribes or agencies. Previous studies have found that there are more than twice as many small tribal police departments (those with less than nine officers) than there are medium-sized (10–45) or large (over 100) departments. Any police department must reach at least a minimum size in order to cover shifts (generally two officers for each of three shifts) regardless of the population for which it is responsible. Small departments may serve substantially fewer people, which could easily skew

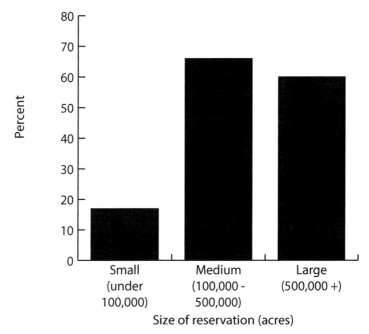

Figure 5.2. Tribes with 911 emergency response systems in 2000.

the statistics.[22] Another factor could be that the chronic shortage may not be a result of a lack of personnel per se but a lack of adequate personnel relative to the geographic size of the community and/or inadequate resources (e.g., a lack of 911 systems or an insufficient number of vehicles) that prevents departments from effectively serving the community.

A complicating factor for tribal law enforcement is the attrition rate for new officers. The ICLEI report asserts that, according to the Indian Police Academy, the attrition rate of new officers during its sixteen-week training program is approximately 50 percent. Further complicating this attrition problem is the fact that approximately 50 percent of those officers who complete the IPA training leave Indian Country law enforcement within two years.[23]

Given the reported inadequacy of police services in Indian Country, it is notable that a Harvard Criminal Justice Policy study entitled "Policing on American Indian Reservations," published in 2000, found that only fifty percent of the tribal police departments reported participating in a 911 emergency telephone system.[24] My own data, compiled in 2000, were broken down into small, medium, and large reservations (see fig. 5.2). It revealed that more than half of the medium and large reservations had 911 systems, but only 18 percent of the small reservations had them. The problem of the vast patrol area that each officer is responsible for is undoubtedly compounded by the lack of such a system.

Personnel Policies

A significant percentage of the tribal law enforcement agencies responding to the 2000 study (41.1 percent) pay their patrol officers an average of ten dollars per hour or less (see fig. 5.3). It is difficult to assess the adequacy of this pay rate, however. Although this rate would be extremely low for non-Indian agencies, it must be measured against the levels of poverty and unemployment faced by those living in Indian Country. A comparison with these figures indicates that tribal police may be among the privileged few to have adequately paid employment.[25]

While the pay levels may be relatively low, the tribal police departments do provide benefits that are common to law enforcement in the non-Indian community. Ninety percent of all agencies provide sworn officers with life insurance, 65 percent provide retirement benefits, and 92 percent provide annual leave.

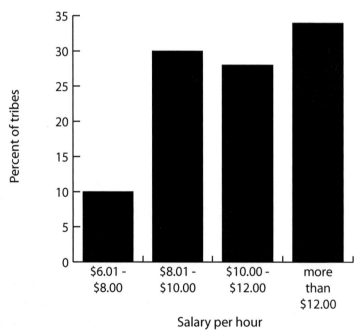

Figure 5.3. Average salary of officers in responding tribal police departments in 2000.

While the educational level on many reservations is very low,[26] the tribal law enforcement agencies uniformly require at least a high school diploma or a general equivalency diploma for employment. Only one tribe reported not requiring a high school diploma. This educational requirement is consistent with the majority of rural, and even urban, police departments in the United States.

An additional factor for American Indian tribal police departments is their obvious preference for hiring Indian people for sworn positions. Although only 10 percent of the agencies reported requiring tribal membership for new employees, the vast majority (85.5 percent) reported having a Native American preference for new employees.

The issue arises as to the legal propriety of tribal governments having a hiring preference for Native Americans. While the Indian Civil Rights Act, codified as 25 USC Sec. 1301–1303 (as amended) states that "no Indian tribe in exercising powers of self-government shall . . . deny to any person within its jurisdiction the equal protection of its laws or deprive any person of liberty or property without due process of law," this has not interfered with the legal right, pursuant to case law, of a tribal government to establish a Native American preference for hiring.[27]

Operational Policies

American Indian tribal police departments and those local law enforcement agencies that abut reservations have significant jurisdictional issues to overcome if they hope to provide quality service to Indian peoples. With rural and tribal law enforcement strained due to wide geographic dispersal and limited 911 services, the ability to provide adequate service and enhance officer safety can depend upon good working relationships between local and tribal law enforcement. Unfortunately, these good relationships do not always exist. Given the recent establishment of most tribal police departments and the informality with which many operate, the development of a comprehensive written body of policies and procedures is critical.

Written Policies and Procedures
Most of the tribal police departments have formalized written procedures, although some simply have collections of standing orders that serve as protocols. Nearly all the responding tribal police departments (93.4 percent) have a written policy on the use of deadly force by their officers, and a little more than half (55.7 percent) of those policies set defense of life as the standard. Most agencies (82.3 percent) have a written policy on handling

domestic violence incidents, and two-thirds (66.1 percent) of those policies have a mandatory-arrest standard. Almost all agencies (93.5 percent) have a formal procedure for handling community complaints against their officers, and one-fifth (21.3 percent) have a community review board for handling such complaints. Only 13 percent, however, have a brochure explaining the complaint process. These systems vary from tribe to tribe, but all fall within the general structures common in the non-Indian community. The tribal accountability systems generally rely on investigations of misconduct done by the police departments themselves. The findings of these investigations are then reviewed by boards of tribal community members who may comment on the adequacy of the findings and in some cases may hold their own hearings on the allegations of wrongdoing.

Community Policing in Indian Country

The pursuit of tribal sovereignty and self-government necessitates the development of democratic institutions within tribal governments that are both adequate and accountable.[28] If these institutions are not accountable or do not meet the needs of tribal members, they can do more harm than good. Tribal police departments, given their importance in the maintenance of law and order and the protection of tribal members, cannot be allowed to fit into the latter category. They must be both culturally compatible and effective in reducing crime and in providing law enforcement services to a largely underserved population. The question is how this can best be done.

To truly meet the needs of Indian people, tribal police departments must be carefully planned and implemented to fit each community and the challenges it faces.[29] They must be accountable to the tribal government to ensure that any defects in the original design, staffing, or operations can be corrected as they become apparent.

As discussed earlier in this chapter, the concept of community policing is easily applicable to Indian Country. This approach to policing is based on the concepts of restorative justice and the enhancement of community cohesion and action, ideas that fit well within Indian Country.

In 1997 the Community Policing Consortium (CPC) produced a report entitled "To Protect and Serve: An Overview of Community Policing on Indian Reservations." This report was the result of a study of seventeen tribal police departments. It called attention to the shift in Indian Country law enforcement from a call-for-service model to a community-policing model. Arguably, given the personnel and infrastructure challenges facing tribal law enforcement, a community policing approach can be more efficient than the professional model.

Community policing, with its crime prevention approach and its emphasis on community support and problem solving, can ease community concerns in a way that emphasizing answering calls for service and crime fighting does not. The report noted that the community is more supportive when it sees the law enforcement as trying to solve a problem, rather than simply engaging in punitive behavior.[30] Under community policing, officers are no longer recognized mainly for their arrest and citation records but are expected to use their discretion in many circumstances to produce an outcome in the best interests of all involved.

The community policing approach of proactive peacekeeping emphasizes officers' responsibility and accountability to the community rather than only to the department's chain of command. The devolution of power to, and consultation with, a broad-based circle of responsible leaders is a common approach to decision making in many Indian communities. This element alone could greatly enhance the work of police in Indian communities.

The CPC report found that the tribal law enforcement programs surveyed had a number of practices in common.[31] Among these were the following:

- initiating crime prevention programs and initiatives, including safety and public awareness campaigns, Drug Abuse Resistance Education (DARE) programs, and Just Say No programs;
- assigning special officers to work on gang control and to work with juveniles and children in single-parent households or to act as community liaisons (with, in some cases, each district, community, or village having a designated officer who lives there);
- attending meetings with community leaders and community members;
- requiring officers to attend formal community meetings and social or cultural events;
- working with public housing program staff, drug and alcohol counselors, mental health professionals, health service staff, and the staff at schools;
- providing mediation, dispute resolution, and other problem-solving techniques directly or in cooperation with local agencies that provide these services — for example, a peace court or designated community member who resolves conflicts (referred to in the report as a "mayordomo");

- emphasizing the service side of law enforcement, such as jump-starting cars, unlocking car doors, and delivering urgent messages;
- reinforcing a professional demeanor for officers, including treating community members with respect rather than trying to intimidate them;
- emphasizing rapid response to calls and a thoroughly professional performance, including preparing a complete and accurate report;
- developing an internal-affairs division, humanizing the department, and demonstrating the expectation that officers will follow professional standards and that allegations of a violation of these standards will be investigated to help to break down the us-versus-them attitude that can develop between the department and the community;
- and establishing and reinforcing a good working relationship with nearby law enforcement agencies.

Many of these characteristic activities depend very much on the situation facing an agency at a given time. Usually tribal law enforcement departments are constrained by time, personnel, or financial and infrastructure challenges. While a given department may see the promise in a community policing approach and may even be able to allocate some resources, the exigencies of crime in Indian Country are such that priorities easily change, and long-term problem solving may easily take a backseat to resolving an immediate crisis.

One criticism often levied against community policing systems, with their emphasis on devolution of authority and decision making from the top of the hierarchy to lower-level officers, is that the resultant reduction in centralized control can also lead to a lack of appropriate accountability. In order to overcome this danger, tribal police departments should develop clear rules and protocols for officers to follow, thus alleviating the tendency to make up rules as questions arise.

Reflections

Tribal police departments are perfectly positioned to reflect the best in American policing. The concept of community policing, newly embraced in mainstream policing, is a natural for tribal police departments as well. They are close to their communities, they generally reflect the diversity of those communities, and they are in the early stages of development. The importance of the last characteristic cannot be overstated. In newer departments, bad habits and a tolerance for misconduct have not yet had the opportunity to become deeply rooted. Today, tribal police departments are thus at a critical stage in their development. Making the correct decisions now will be of great significance for the development of tribal police programs in the future, as well as for the enhancement of tribal sovereignty and self-governance.

An essential element in developing responsive and accountable tribal police departments is the process of tribes moving away from having law enforcement provided by the BIA. In recent years, an increasing number of tribes are establishing and extending tribal police services rather than continuing to rely on law enforcement services provided by the BIA-LES. When the tribe develops its own police department, it is directed by the tribal council rather than a federal agency. Tribal police are tribal personnel who are accountable to the tribal community. Tribal codes and ordinances developed by the police department are reflective of the tribe's needs and vision rather than the needs of the federal government. The tribe is free to decide on the style and mode of policing that it wants and to ensure that this form of policing takes place in Indian Country.

Through the use of PL 93-638 contracts and self-governance funding, tribes can provide their own police services while still using federal funds. Thus, police services can be what the tribes want them to be, without being an overwhelming burden on the tribal budget.

6 Training Tribal Law Enforcement Personnel

Training law enforcement personnel is essential if police officers are to be able to work with and for their communities. This is a challenge that faces all police agencies. It is difficult to keep up with changes in technology and laws while also coping with the recruitment, hiring, and development of new personnel and with the training of existing personnel for present assignments and opportunities for promotion. When these challenges are combined with other problems inherent in tribal policing — including minimal budgets, low pay scales, the attrition of trained personnel, a scarcity of new or existing technology, and the need to understand the complexity of tribal cultures and the dynamics of violence in native communities — it is truly amazing that tribal police departments have grown and prospered, and have found ways to meet the challenge of protecting and serving while retaining their cultural compatibility.

There are various types of tribal law enforcement training. Some is for state or federal certification, and officers in this type of training can be cross-deputized with surrounding agencies or with federal law enforcement. This training is generally conducted on-site at a training academy. Other training is aimed at continuing education, which is necessary to retaining certification and/or to enhance an officer's professional knowledge and abilities. Continuing-education training can be done at a training site or conference, or through videos or the Internet. Yet another form of training is site specific and develops knowledge of and competency in tribal rules, regulations, protocols, codes, and ordinances. Finally, some tribes encourage tribal police officers to obtain formal education at the university or community college level. Often, as with the Navajo Nation, formal education is linked to promotional opportunities.

Training new officers and maintaining and enhancing the training of existing officers is a challenge in Indian Country, where the attrition rate is high and many officers are recent hires. Because of the high rates of turnover experienced by many tribal police departments, training must be done in a manner that ensures that a person does not leave the department without passing on the knowledge obtained. This necessitates the development of written tribal procedures and protocols and of a training infrastructure that can protect the body of essential knowledge.

Many tribes wish to have their law enforcement personnel cross-deputized with state law enforcement agencies, which requires individual officers to be state certified. State certification in turn requires that the officer complete a course of training at a state-certified academy. This raises a cultural or professional issue for some tribes, as they want their officers to adhere to tribal cultural values and modes of behavior rather than the ways and values of law enforcement generally. The training at the Indian Police Academy meets the desire of tribes to have officers federally certified and trained in up-to-date policing techniques within Indian Country and with an acknowledgement of Indian values and mores. This approach, however, requires the officers to complete their course of training at the Indian Police Academy itself, which is housed at the Federal Law Enforcement Training Center (FLETC) in Artesia, New Mexico.

Either of these courses of law enforcement academy training requires a significant investment of time and resources for tribal governments, which can be a barrier to training in many instances. Although the Indian Police Academy is the gold standard for tribal law enforcement, tribes often conduct training in-house or send officers to local training seminars on specific issues because they cannot spare the personnel or the expense.

Training is developed and conducted in many ways in Indian Country. Some tribes rely on tribal personnel, others on state or federal assistance. However training is conducted, the results are generally impressive. Training enhances the ability of an officer to conduct activities in a responsible, respectful, and safe manner, which enhances the respect and support that flows to law enforcement from the community the officer serves. However, training conducted by tribal personnel or at the Indian Police Academy does not meet the requirements for state certification even if it is equal to any other training received. One idea to explore is to make tribal-officer training reciprocal with the Arizona Peace Officer Standards and Training Board (POST), thus allowing tribal officers to meet the conditions for state certification while remaining within Indian Country.

Training at the Colorado River Indian Tribes Reservation

A close examination of the reservation of the Colorado River Indian Tribes (CRIT), centered in Parker, Arizona, reveals the extent of the problems faced by Indian nations when they seek to fulfill their law enforcement mission. Unlike many tribal police departments, the CRIT department has existed for many years. The reservation land lies in both California and Arizona and includes law enforcement jurisdiction in both states as well as over a portion of the Colorado River.

Prior to the 1970s there was no training specifically for tribal law enforcement. This changed in 1975 when CRIT officers began attending the Indian Police Academy. In the 1980s the CRIT tribal police department also began to send officers to the Southern Arizona Law Enforcement Training Center. Now all officers are state certified. CRIT requires six weeks of field training for new officers after sixteen weeks at the state academy. These requirements may be waived for officers who have been employed elsewhere prior to employment with CRIT. Eight hours of advanced officer training is required every three years for state certification. The Bureau of Indian Affairs requires an additional two weeks of training in federal criminal laws for the issuance of the BIA Certification Commission card.

Training of new officers is a fairly constant activity, as there is a turnover rate of one to two years. The high turnover rate is attributed to a number of factors, including pay scales, lack of promotional opportunity, and lack of state retirement benefits. Officers who leave generally go to other tribal police departments that pay better and have more benefits.

The majority of officers are non-Indian, but since most applicants are from Arizona, they are generally familiar with tribes and reservations, so that is not seen as a problem. Generally, a new officer who is not yet certified is required to attend the state academy within three months of employment. Thus, CRIT seeks applicants who are already state certified. If not state certified, the officer accompanies a sworn officer on the job as a civilian observer. They are on paid status and are given badges.

CRIT has one officer who is designated as a training sergeant. Training is based on individual needs and on the department's need for specialization. CRIT attempts to honor specific requests for training on topics of interest; however, a lack of staffing can preclude attendance off-reservation. CRIT officers attend training programs organized by local cities and counties and conduct training that other departments attend. They also have squad room training via a satellite hookup to POST.

The CRIT field training component is tailored to the needs of the tribal community and the officer. It includes material on reservation and legal jurisdictional issues, tribal codes, call handling, decision making, and officer safety. The field training officer (FTO) preplans with the trainee prior to answering a call. At the end of each day a critique sheet is prepared and discussed. In the third week of employment, the trainee begins to handle calls, with the FTO as backup. During the fourth week, the FTO attends calls in civilian clothes as an observer. At the end of each day, the trainee completes reports and the FTO reviews them. While the academy covers the writing of police reports, the field training program emphasizes their legal sufficiency. Reports are rewritten by the trainee if necessary. The FTO prepares a written evaluation on each trainee at the end of the six-week field training program. A number of trainees have not successfully passed the field training program and have left the department.

The Bureau of Indian Affairs requires forty hours of training for federal certification; however, they recognize any formal or informal training (e.g., via satellite hookup) as meeting this requirement. The BIA criminal investigator assigned to this region, who provides extended investigative services for any federal or major crime, conducts or oversees the forty hours of required in-service training for a number of tribes, including CRIT, Fort Mojave, Cocopah, Chemehuevi, and the Quechan tribe of the Fort Yuma Reservation.

The BIA criminal investigator places special emphasis on criminal evidence and crime scene control, the role of first responders, interviewing, and report writing. He asserts that tribal officers handle incidents of violent physical assault and domestic violence very well, and that, compared to mainstream officers, tribal officers are especially adept at de-escalating violent incidents. He contends, however, that Indian Country police supervisors need special training in reviewing reports for legal sufficiency and in writing and thinking clearly. Thus, all their reports should be reviewed, as officers without much formal education often lack the ability to set out clearly the elements of the crime asserted.

The CRIT tribal attorney general prosecutes tribal arrests and transmits major crime reports to the federal courts. He also conducts training for the CRIT tribal police department, with officers from the county sheriff's office or city police included by request. The attorney general contends that CRIT tribal police are well trained in the use of force and in the de-escalation of violent incidents. Their primary training issue is the handling of evidence and first-responder responsibilities. He further contends that essential elements of the crime asserted are often missed in reports. He has conducted training explicitly on these issues, as well as on tribal codes and laws. He believes that the officers know Arizona codes and laws well, as these are emphasized at the state academy, but that tribal codes and laws require specific training at the tribal level.

CRIT officers contend that most of their cases involve alcohol. The officers estimate that in approximately 90 percent of the calls someone is drunk. This then results in domestic violence, assaults, and other crimes. There are many calls related to guns and drugs, and many others related to child molestation. They assert that there is a need for training in interpersonal communication and in defensive tactics. CRIT officers further contend that training in basic techniques and procedures is needed on a continuing basis. They believe that officers would welcome continuing education, particularly if special recognition or benefits were attached. This is supported by the fact that individual officers have undertaken the development of specific tribal policies and protocols and have served as trainers for CRIT and other police departments. CRIT officers undertook these activities without financial compensation, considering the community and professional recognition to be sufficient reward.

State Police Academies

Training programs conducted by state police academies conform to the standards set forth by the POST program. The academies are regional in nature, with officers living in the dorms if their home department is more than thirty-five miles from the academy. An example of a regional POST training program is the Southern Arizona Law Enforcement Training Center (SALETC) in Tucson, Arizona. A state-certified academy that is in full accordance with Arizona POST, SALETC trains officers from around the state.

Incoming SALETC training classes have about fifty to sixty members, although this number has ranged from eleven to seventy-three. The training program for state certification is sixteen weeks long and covers the whole range of training (e.g., classroom training in the law, lectures regarding proper procedures, and proficiency training, including firearms and driving). The training is not culturally specific and does not address tribal community expectations for law enforcement. An important factor in POST training is that courses are routinely accepted as transfer credits by community colleges toward associate of arts degrees. The credits earned in obtaining these degrees can then be transferred to a college or university if an officer wishes to pursue advanced education.

SALETC often receives trainees from tribal police departments, but it is fairly common for these officers to fail to complete the sixteen-week course of training. The majority of officers who leave do so voluntarily, citing the difficulties inherent in being away from home. SALETC does not question officers who choose to leave voluntarily but asserts that, along with finding it difficult to be away from home, the officers sometimes find the training to be different from what they had expected. However, contributing factors could also include the fact that state certification is not generally required for tribal officers, and they are usually able to continue in their positions and to obtain training at the tribal or federal level, which may better conform to their native values and mores.

In-House Training

In many of the tribal communities evaluated, the training of law enforcement officers is conducted by the tribal prosecutor's office. The training is legalistic and the emphasis is on presenting information from the victim's point of view. A number of issues are addressed that are not commonly covered in a police academy, and the training tends to be very culturally specific and, according to the participants and trainers, is highly successful.

In regard to domestic violence, for example, the training attempts to help officers understand why women might return to their abusers and also focuses on other charges besides assault and battery that could be levied against a perpetrator. Prior to the training, officers were surveyed. Their attitudes toward domestic violence situations were generally negative. Many considered it a waste of time to develop a domestic violence case. Over the course of training, however, the officers' attitudes became more positive, and this positive attitude was retained with continuing training.

The Indian Police Academy

As noted above, the Indian Police Academy is housed, along with other law enforcement training programs, at the FLETC. It is a sixteen-week residential training program for tribal law enforcement, including fish-and-game officers and firefighters. During the fall of 2003 I visited the training program, where I attended classes, surveyed the entering and graduating trainees, and evaluated the training for the faculty and administration of the academy. The information in this section results from that site visit.

The entering class for the Indian Police Academy generally consists of fifty officers. The attrition rate is approximately 10 to 15 percent. Those officers who left training did so for both academic and disciplinary reasons.

According to the academy, more than 70 percent of the Indian Police Academy trainees have a high school diploma, approximately 2 percent have some college education, and some have vocational training. Approximately 18 percent are ex-military, more than 25 percent have family members with law enforcement service, and 10 percent have a family history of firefighting.

The rules of the academy are strict, and life is very structured. The academy is conducted in a paramilitary format, with an express chain of command. There is an emphasis on marching in formation and tight discipline. Class participants are required to march into the classroom as a unit. This differs from other academies conducted at FLETC, where officers are allowed to drink at the facility (there is a bar on site), and discipline is generally more lax.

Women are required to march, do push-ups, and participate in other conditioning activities, such as climbing stairs regardless of their menstrual cycle. There is mandatory one-hour study hall each evening. No one may leave the center during the first few weeks of training. No drinking of alcohol is allowed at the center, and morning formation in full uniform is at 6:15. Surprise room inspections are conducted, and push-ups are required if rooms are not neat. All squad members must do push-ups, for example, if a participant forgets his or her hat.

The academy instructors model expected behavior to the officers. They refer to each other, and to the officers, as sir and ma'am. They emphasize respect of the rights and values of others, including those who may be wrongdoers. As one instructor emphasized, "It could be you in that [jail] facility." This training attitude of Indian Police Academy trainees stands in stark contrast to that of other agency trainees at the FLETC, who were overheard laughing about "stomping some illegals."

The Indian Police Academy instructors placed an emphasis on integrity, fairness, and honesty. It was stated explicitly that even the appearance of impropriety was improper. During one class there was a discussion about whether it was allowable to lie to a suspect. The class consensus was that this was acceptable, which was then emphatically contradicted by the instructor. As another instructor stated to the officers, "You are a viable professional. You have a critical role in the community." It is this pride in themselves as officers and in their role in their communities that the instructors hope will be internalized by the officers.

Teaching techniques varied widely. Some of the instructors were very interactive, with an emphasis on class participation and dialogue. These were generally low tech, with an emphasis on writing on the board at the front of the classroom. Others lectured in a very structured style, with written and PowerPoint materials that were strictly followed. In these classes there was little voluntary class participation. While most of the instructors frequently used examples from Indian Country, a few did not. This was attributed to the fact that most of the instructors were recent recruits from positions in Indian Country, while others had been out of the field for ten years or more.

As part of this site visit during the fall of 2003, I conducted two surveys of trainees. The entering class consisted of forty-three trainees, representing twenty-seven tribal law enforcement agencies. I surveyed this class at the end of the third week of training. The exiting class consisted of thirty-four trainees, representing twenty-two tribal law enforcement agencies. I surveyed this class during the last week of their training. In all, a total of seventy-seven trainees responded to the survey, but not all of them responded to all the questions. There were also three focus group discussions, and seven officers volunteered to be interviewed individually.

I asked all of the trainees about their prior employment and training, and their time on the job prior to attending the academy. Each class was asked about the types of training they had received from their employing tribe prior to entering the academy, and the entering trainees were asked about what training they thought they needed. The exiting trainees were asked to rate the quality of the training they had received at the academy and what additional training might be necessary.

The results of the surveys indicated that most of the trainees had been on the job an average of seven and a half months prior to their attendance at the Indian Police Academy. This time period varied widely, however, from one week to five years, with thirteen of the sixty respondents to this question having been on the job for more than a year.

Only twenty-one of the seventy-seven trainees responded that they had experience in policing prior to their employment with their present tribal police agency, and twelve indicated that they had state certification. Of the twenty-one with prior experience, ten had been either city or state officers, nine had been employed as officers with other tribal police departments, and two had been in BIA law enforcement. It was generally those trainees who had been state or city police who also had state certification.

The entering trainees generally responded that the three activities with the highest priority for law enforcement on their reservations were emergency calls, drug and alcohol enforcement, and domestic violence. This was confirmed by the exiting trainees, with few of either group thinking that community education, crime prevention, or fostering community partnerships and collaboration were a high priority for their agencies. The entering trainees generally specified that they were hoping for academy training in the handling of domestic violence and child abuse and neglect cases, in crime analysis and investigation, and in defensive techniques. Many stated that they believed that community relations training was essential for their jobs as tribal police officers.

The exiting trainees were asked to rate the individual class training they had received at the academy. The Indian law class was rated the highest, with comments made about the high quality of the instructor, her evident concern that they understand the material, and her positive reinforcement. Other classes that were rated high included accident investigation, officer safety and defensive driving techniques, domestic violence, and use of firearms and nonlethal force. The officers believed that additional training was needed on road and water rescue training and drug identification. In general, the officers stated that they believed that the Indian Police Academy had met the expectations they had when they came to the academy.

Criticisms of the academy focused on the desire for instructors to treat the trainees as adults and to criticize them in a constructive manner. Twenty-seven of thirty-one respondents indicated that instructors focused more on mistakes made by the trainees than on their successes.

Training Conducted by the Indian Country Inter-tribal Network

The Indian Country Intelligence Network (ICIN), a project of the International Association of Chiefs of Police, is a national organization that focuses specifically on the development and enhancement of tribal police departments. It serves as a network organization to discuss issues that challenge tribal law enforcement, as well as specific changes in laws, grant opportunities, and improvements in technology.

ICIN training is on officer-involved shootings and other aspects of law enforcement. The training includes the responsibilities that tribal police have to the BIA-LES and also what responses tribal police departments may expect from tribal governments. There are also discussions about appropriate responses to demands made by others.

The implementation of data collection and tracking programs is emphasized. Many tribal police departments lack efficient and effective computer-based data tracking systems. ICIN emphasizes the need for such equipment and for training of law enforcement personnel in their value and use.

ICIN also serves as a clearinghouse for new legal requirements for law enforcement. At one meeting ICIN discussed tribal sovereignty and emphasized the need to fully develop tribal police departments. They reviewed the legal requirements of search warrants, discussed issues related to the bureaucratic delay in the issuance of BIA Certification Commission cards, discussed procedural issues related to the provision of police services through a PL 93-638 contract, and provided clarification of the ability of tribal law enforcement to arrest non-Indian perpetrators through application of the federal PATRIOT Act.

Training in a Specific Area: Domestic Violence

Domestic violence threatens the whole fabric of the Indian community and thus is a focus of the attention of law enforcement. It is an area where there is active code development and implementation, but it is also an area where surveyed officers believed more training is necessary. Therefore, it is important to take a close look at tribal police training in the field of domestic violence.

The results from the 1996–2000 STOP Violence Against Indian Women (STOP VAIW) evaluation indicated that the tribes were outspoken in their belief that more training in the field of domestic violence would greatly enhance the law enforcement response. The data suggested that the most successful training method was mandatory training conducted by criminal justice personnel, including specialized officers, tribal prosecutors, and consultants with law enforcement backgrounds.[1]

The evaluation study found that a collaborative effort by relevant law enforcement agencies, both tribal and nontribal, is essential if domestic violence is to be controlled in Indian Country. The largest contributor to poor interagency collaboration was found to be a lack of training in how best to respond to criminal conduct.

To address this lack of training, more than 75 percent of the tribal departments queried during the STOP VAIW evaluation developed and conducted training. Some tribes took it upon themselves to implement training for law enforcement personnel, judges, prosecutors, health service providers, and advocates. In other cases it was individual agencies, such as the domestic violence program, that organized training sessions for other agencies. Domestic violence training is conducted at the Indian Police Academy and is also the focus of special in-service training symposiums conducted by consultants and inter-tribal organizations. This training is conducted in a variety of ways:

- agency personnel were sent outside the community for federal, state, or county training with a nonnative emphasis;
- agency personnel participated in training conducted by Indian Country consultants in an intertribal format;

- national native resource centers were invited to send staff members to a tribal community to train various agencies;
- the Indian Police Academy included a specific unit on the law as it relates to domestic violence and the procedures for handling domestic violence incidents; and
- a training curriculum was developed and implemented within the community itself.

There was considerable debate over which types of training are most effective. The evaluation indicated that the personnel of many agencies, such as law enforcement, prefer to be trained by colleagues rather than by someone outside their discipline. The evaluation further established that the courses of training developed and implemented by a tribal community tended to be more culturally specific than those developed from outside the community.

Domestic Violence Training by Tribal Personnel

An example of tribal training regarding domestic violence is that conducted by the Eastern Band of the Cherokee. This tribe provided the Cherokee police department officers with this training twice over a four-month period. After the trainings the officers who participated were asked to voluntarily fill out a posttraining survey. These responses, while ostensibly responding to questions about the domestic violence training, were more global in nature. Some of the results were as follows:

- The need for collaboration of community efforts and agencies was recognized.
- There was recognition of the need for more education given to professionals and the community in general.
- Officers found particularly useful: information on evidence, interview, and investigation details to include in reports, and lethality assessment.
- Others requested training in why officers may hold the views they do and what their cohorts can do to change the prevailing attitudes.
- The officers requested more training in legal changes, evidence collection, and report writing.

Domestic Violence Training by Indian Country Consultants

Given the recognition of the pervasiveness of domestic violence in Indian Country, a number of consultant groups have been awarded contracts by the federal government and some tribes to train tribal government members and law enforcement personnel in the relevant law and procedures. Many of these groups specifically focus on the training of tribal law enforcement personnel, including tribal police, judges, prosecutors, public defenders, and victim assistants. They emphasize the handling of arrests and evidence, report writing, the elements of the crime, and the development of appropriate protocols and ordinances. They also focus on background investigations, the legal sufficiency of search warrants, and interview techniques.

Generally, the consultants emphasize the need for law enforcement departments to collaborate and to share information. This can be of particular importance due to the small size and complicated jurisdictional issues facing most tribal police departments. They also emphasize the need for a full range of law enforcement options, including tribal courts and probation systems. This in itself is a useful component to the training program, as many tribes do not have courts or systems of accountability, such as probation officers.

The Stalking Resource Center and the Native American Circle conduct training for Indian Country law enforcement personnel under contract to the Victims of Crime Office of the U.S. Department of Justice. This training is offered free of charge to tribal groups such as ICIN. The trainers emphasize that tribal courts and tribal probation officers can seriously affect law-and-order code violators' compliance with court orders. They emphasized that, prior to the development of a probation system, 80 percent of tribal law-and-order code violators were not held accountable, leaving them to re-offend at will. After one year of operation of an accountability system (i.e., formal probation), more than 50 percent of tribal code violators were in compliance with probation orders, and 50 percent did not re-offend.

Yet another training consultant under contract to the U.S. Department of Justice is the Southwest Center for Law and Policy (SWCLAP). This organization, predominantly staffed by American Indian law enforcement professionals and by professionals with long experience working in tribal settings, conducts training of tribal law enforcement and also develops codes and protocols for specific tribes. I serve on the board of directors of SWCLAP.

The training of tribal law enforcement officers is conducted in multitribal groups through the National Tribal Trial College (NTTC), for which I am a faculty member. NTTC is sponsored by SWCLAP and is a joint effort of SWCLAP and Arizona POST and is funded through a grant from the U.S. Department of Justice. The NTTC conducts large-scale training courses four times a year in various regions of the United States and also conducts site visits to provide training to tribes at their request. Also upon the request of a specific tribe, the NTTC can develop and/or review codes and protocols related to domestic violence, sexual assault, elder and child abuse, and stalking.

NTTC training sessions focus on tribal justice personnel, including tribal prosecutors and defense attorneys, advocates, judges, and law enforcement personnel. Evaluations by participants of all SWCLAP training presentations are done at each event. SWCLAP training differs from the traditional sixteen-week law enforcement academy approach because SWCLAP has found that training of tribal law enforcement personnel is best done in short segments on a frequent basis. It has also found that including all tribal justice personnel in training sessions helps each to understand the challenges faced by the others.

Tribal participants in SWCLAP training emphasize the importance of the training clearly differentiating between the challenges facing Indian Country and those facing mainstream communities. They especially appreciate it when the trainers give Indian-specific examples and tell stories rather than lecturing in a linear fashion. They further found those sessions that allow for open-ended discussions and that contained problem-solving components to be the most valuable.

I conducted a survey of tribal law enforcement trainees at NTTC training in 2004. Approximately half of the law enforcement officers who registered for the training returned survey forms. The results of the survey indicated that tribal officers preferred training by law enforcement practitioners who were part of, or familiar with, Indian Country, such as that provided by NTTC. As one officer stated, NTTC instructors "can relate to real issues." Another stated that, while the elements of a crime are the same in mainstream and tribal jurisdictions, the trainees appreciated the NTTC training in jurisdictional issues in Indian Country and in the working of tribal courts. Yet another respondent stated that NTTC provided a "less stressful environment" in which to learn. The NTTC respondents overwhelmingly stated that they would like to attend other NTTC training sessions and specifically requested training in jurisdictional issues, changes in current laws and their effect on reservations, and investigative skills.

Nontribal organizations, such as county sheriffs and state police, frequently attend the SWCLAP training. Their evaluation responses supported the opportunity to train alongside tribal law enforcement personnel. Both tribal and nontribal participants responded that training together helped each to understand the other. The training was rated excellent or good by an overwhelming majority of the participants.

Reflections

The training conducted by tribally specific agencies is different from that conducted by mainstream training programs. When queried about these differences, officers participating in tribally focused programs noted the following characteristics of tribally specific training:

- an emphasis on wisdom and the exercise of discretion in a manner that focused on Indian communities;
- an emphasis on information needed for day-to-day work and a hands-on approach;
- a less stressful environment, resulting from tribal officers being trained together and an emphasis on Indian Country issues;
- trainers who are Indians themselves and/or who are involved in and knowledgeable about Indian Country.

These differences have ramifications. Often tribal officers are not viewed as regular police by mainstream police officers. They are seen as not having the level of skill or knowledge that a state-trained officer would have and may be viewed as similar to security guards. The question is whether these training differences enhance policing at the tribal level or hinder it, and the answer is critical if tribal police departments are to meet the needs of the tribal communities.

Unfortunately, a complication for tribal departments is that an emphasis on training and, in particular, formal education encourages head-hunting by nontribal law enforcement agencies, which often attempt to recruit Indian officers. While this enhances the opportunities for individuals, it makes it difficult for tribal police departments to retain valuable employees. A discussion of this problem occurred at Navajo Nation recently when a female lieutenant was promoted to captain. She has remained at Navajo Nation even in the face of many offers from nontribal departments.[2] A highly trained, formally educated, experienced officer is a prize for any department. It is a challenge for tribal departments, particularly in the face of short staffing and low pay, to retain such valuable employees. The answer is not, however, to restrict training or to fail to encourage education and accomplishment; rather, the answer is for Indian Country to find ways to reward such officers and to encourage their retention and promotion.

7
Infrastructure Challenges

The provision of police service to reservation residents is of critical concern to tribal governments. Rapidity of response to calls for service is one of the hallmarks of competent policing. A quick response to an emergency call engenders confidence that a crime will be addressed and brings relief to victims even if the officer does nothing but take a report. In Indian Country, however, obstacles to rapid response are significant.

Much of Indian Country is rural, with settlements and villages widely spaced. Often the roads between settled areas are unpaved and difficult to pass in inclement weather. The terrain may be mountainous, or there may be geographic characteristics that impede radio or cell phone communication. These issues are compounded when tribal law enforcement personnel and infrastructure issues are factored into the equation. Law enforcement in Indian Country often lacks basic elements that are taken for granted in mainstream policing. Adequate budgets and trained personnel may be difficult to achieve, 911 systems are often unavailable, and dependable police cars can be scarce. Additionally, tribal police officers generally work without partners, and backup can be very far away from a call for service (see table 7.1).

During the 1990s seventeen reservation officers lost their lives in the line of duty. This number is extremely high; in fact, tribal officers are four times as likely to be killed as other police.[1] Ted Quasula, past head of the Bureau of Indian Affairs Law Enforcement Services, has attributed this loss of life to a lack of staffing, one-person shifts, the need to work double shifts, and patrolling that is far from backup. He stated, "What really makes this painful is that if you go anywhere outside the reservation, if an officer goes on a dangerous call, there is backup."[2] A number of officers have also been killed falling asleep at the wheel of their police car.

Studies conducted by the BIA-LES indicated that 2,300 officers work on tribal land. The BIA found that an additional 4,300 are needed to provide basic law enforcement services to reservations, but there may not be adequate funding available to hire them. In 1999 tribal law enforcement received a $20 million increase, for a total of $157 million. However, Mr. Quasula projected that it would take approximately $500 million to adequately police Indian Country.[3]

An additional complicating factor is an inability to hire and train tribal police personnel. Due to low pay rates, high attrition rates, and the dangerous nature of the job, it is difficult to recruit and train officers. Furthermore, it is common for tribal officers, once they receive their training and gain some experience, to transfer to police officer positions in surrounding agencies, where the pay and working conditions are better.

Yet another critical concern is the fact that tribal officers often are placed in jeopardy due to inadequate staffing and the inability of tribes to field two-person cars or to ensure adequate cover for an officer forced to work alone. This lack of staffing, combined with a lack of cars and radios, can endanger tribal officers and exacerbate attrition.

To adequately assess the impact of population and calls for service, a number of issues must be closely examined. The area that must be patrolled, the presence of a tribal gaming facility, and the likelihood that police service is provided as part of routine patrol rather than an emergency phone call all must be considered. These factors will give a much truer picture than considering solely the numbers of calls for service.

Calls for Service

Though the number of calls for service to a police agency should not be considered in isolation, it can be indicative of the problems inherent in a jurisdiction and the workload of law enforcement. In the 1996 study, sixty-one tribal police departments provided usable survey information, and of those, twenty provided detailed information. The sixty-one tribal departments reported having 827 sworn officers with patrol duties, and they handled more than 267,600 calls for service during 1996. These same tribes reported that their officers made more than 93,350 arrests, although it is not known how many of these arrests were the result of calls for service and how many were officer initiated.

A review of these numbers indicates that in 1996 each officer handled more than 320 calls for service per year and made more than 110 arrests. While these numbers may be low, they are not the full measure of the job of a tribal police officer. The density of population, the area of a reservation, the availability of a dependable police fleet, and the existence of a 911 emergency response system must also be considered.

Twenty tribal agencies provided detailed information regarding the number of calls for service on an average or very busy shift. These tribes were then grouped by the size of the reservation and whether they were urban or rural in nature. Those six tribes whose area was less than 100,000 acres

Table 7.1   Profiles of Selected Tribal Police Departments

Tribe	Area (acres)	Number of officers	Number of service calls	Number of vehicles	Average vehicle age	Number of vehicles out of service	911	Mutual-aid agreement	Cross-deputization agreement
Blackfoot	1.5 million	37	40	12	2	4	yes	yes	no
Standing Rock	847,799	—	20	26	4	6	—	—	—
Tohono O'odham	2.7 million	71	7	27	4	3	yes	—	—
Flathead	1.2 million	17	15	25	2	2	—	no	yes
Navajo	16.0 million	290	75	340	5	34	yes	yes	yes
Nez Perce	750,000	17	14	9	2	0	no	yes	no
Zuni	463,271	19	9	18	4	0	yes	yes	yes
Umatilla	172,140	22	9	5	4	2	yes	no	yes
Turtle Mountain	140,107	22	8	11	2	2	—	—	—
Pyramid Lake	476,689	8	3	9	4	4	yes	no	no
Rocky Boy	115,000	15	50	6	4	1	no	yes	no
Saganaw Chippewa	138,240	23	10	15	4	10	yes	yes	yes
Lummi	21,000	16	12	9	2	0	yes	yes	no
Oneida	7,658	16	12	8	2	0	no	yes	yes
Puyallup	103	16	8	9	5	1	no	yes	yes
Fort Yuma	43,942	7	3	4	5	0	no	yes	yes
Lake de Hambeau	44,919	9	20	6	4	0	no	yes	no
Hoopa	85,455	13	10	8	2	0	no	yes	yes

were categorized as small reservations, with two of these being rural and four urban. The seven reservations that encompassed between 100,000 and 500,000 acres were deemed to be of medium size, with five of these being rural and two urban. The seven whose area exceeded 500,000 acres were designated as large reservations, all of which were rural in nature. The twenty tribes thus categorized employed a total of 658 officers. They reported that they received 171 calls for service on an average shift and 398 on a very busy shift.

If these numbers are accurate, each tribal officer handled less than one call for service per shift even on a very busy day (see fig. 7.1). Each officer was responsible for only two-thirds the total number of people that a municipal officer covers. However, tribal populations are often widely dispersed, and given the average area of American Indian reservations, an officer may take all day to respond to one call for service. Where that officer is the only officer, or one of few on duty, the rest of the reservation may be left without adequate coverage. This problem is dramatically revealed by the study (see fig. 7.2). The large reservations totaled 25,164,906 acres and employed a total of 452 officers, or an average of 55,675 acres (87 square miles) per officer. The medium-size reservations totaled 1,612,656 acres and employed a total of 105 officers, for an average of 15,359 acres (24 square miles) per officer. The smallest reservations totaled 203,077 acres and employed a total of 83 officers, for an average of 2,447 acres (3.8 square miles) per officer.

The question arises as to why the smaller reservations seem to be disproportionately policed. The smallest reservations employed a total of 83 officers and had a total of 63 calls for very busy shifts, an average of 0.76 calls per officer per shift. The largest reservations had a total of 452 officers and 197 calls on a very busy shift, an average of 0.44 calls per officer per shift. Thus the smaller reservations received more calls per officer, perhaps justifying additional staffing. Most of these smaller reservations are located in urban areas and thus may be disproportionately affected by urban problems. Further, five of the six small reservations have gaming facilities, while only three of the seven largest reservations have them. The increased numbers of people present on a reservation with gaming could necessitate a higher

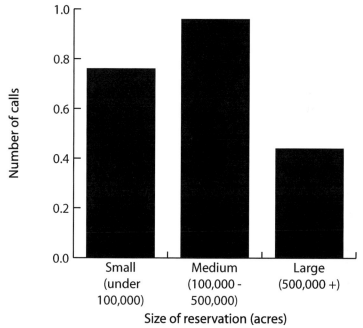

Figure 7.1. Average number of calls for service per officer per shift for responding tribal police departments in 1996.

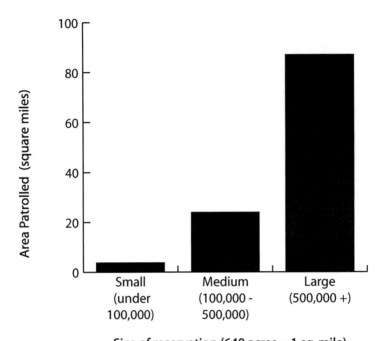

Size of reservation (640 acres = 1 sq. mile)

Figure 7.2. Area patrolled per tribal police officer in 2000.

police presence, helping to explain the higher number of officers employed by smaller reservations.

Patrol Responsibility

Ninety tribes responded to the 2000 survey. This number included fourteen tribes that returned both the 1996 and 2000 surveys. During the study period of 1996–2000, these tribes indicated that their reservations totaled 541,770 in population and 65,468 square miles. They further indicated that from 1996 to 2000 they employed a total of 1,752 sworn officers. These figures reveal that each officer was responsible for an average of 309 people spread over an average reservation size of nearly 40 square miles. This ratio of tribal officers to reservation population compares favorably with the national average of 1 officer per 500 citizens.[4] However, the area to be policed is significantly larger than that covered by a municipal officer.

The rural nature of much of Indian Country can result in additional problems. Cell phone coverage is spotty at best. Cell phone towers do not cover many rural reservation areas. Further, there are many areas where police radios cannot be relied upon. Coverage may be spotty, and in many areas transmissions cannot be heard.

The Navajo Nation is the largest reservation in both population and area in the United States. It encompasses approximately 180,000 people and 25,000 square miles in New Mexico, Utah, and Arizona. A study of the Navajo tribal police department found the following: "As with all officers who patrol rural areas, Navajo officers have to cover many miles alone in a patrol car responding to all types of calls. A detective in Shiprock stated that in mid-1986, 31 officers were responsible for approximately 36,000 people in an area of 4,202 square miles, or one officer for an average of 1,165 people and 135.4 square miles of mostly unpaved roads."[5] The situation has not changed significantly since the 1980s. National law enforcement standards recommend 2 to 2.5 officers for every thousand people. Thus, in mid-1986 there should have been between 72 and 90 officers employed by the Navajo Nation, while instead there were only 31. In 1995 the Navajo Nation had seven Navajo public safety officers patrolling an area of 1.2 million acres and being responsible for 5,800 residents each. By national standards, 12 to 14 officers should have been on patrol.

Since 2003 the Navajo Nation has added 109 new police officers, making a total in 2005 of 351 uniformed officers.[6] This number almost meets the national standard of 1 officer per 450 citizens. The average area for which each officer is responsible was reduced to 71.5 square miles, which is still a huge responsibility, particularly given the nature of the roads, terrain, and number of patrol officers on duty on any particular shift.

To help further improve the patrol situation, the Navajo Nation ordered 92 new police vehicles, for a total of 250 police vehicles, all equipped with laptop computers. In fall 2005 they implemented a Mobile Network Command Center and projected that the dispatchers in each district of the nation would soon have a visual display monitor that would allow for tracking each officer with the Global Positioning System (GPS).[7]

Cooperation with Other Agencies

As discussed in an earlier chapter, mutual-aid agreements with surrounding state and local jurisdictions allow tribal police departments to obtain assistance for its officers in outlying areas, or for tribal police departments to receive law enforcement assistance in cases of emergency. In general, these agreements are rare in Indian Country, and the routine collegiality between fellow officers from different jurisdictions may not exist for tribal officers.

Infrastructure

911 Emergency Response

The ninety tribes surveyed from 1996 to 2000 were asked whether they had a 911 emergency telephone system. Only forty-two reported that they had, with seven reporting that this service was through another agency, generally the county sheriff (see fig. 5.2). The availability of 911 emergency response differed with the nature of the responding tribe. Of the twenty tribes that responded with detailed information, the majority of the large reservations (all of which were rural) had a 911 emergency response capability. However, only one of the six small reservations had one.

Patrol Vehicle Fleets

The tribes that were surveyed in 1996 were asked the number and age of their patrol car fleet. They were also asked how many of these cars were out of service on the day surveyed. Twenty tribal departments responded to this question, although only fifteen of these reported the number of officers employed (see fig. 7.3). One of these tribes reported having 340 patrol cars but only 290 officers. While the number of officers appears to be accurate, the number of cars is questionable. Perhaps the number reflects the total number of tribal administration cars rather than just those assigned to tribal police officers. As it is difficult to factor in this information, it has not been used in this analysis.

Fourteen tribes reported the number of officers and cars, as well as the average age of the fleet and the number of cars out of service on the survey day. These tribes employed a total of 243 officers and had a total of 136 patrol cars, resulting in, at best, approximately one car for every two officers. Thirty-one of these cars were out of service on the survey day, thus only about a hundred were actually available for use. This drops the available vehicles to approximately 1 for every 2.5 officers.

Overall, the nineteen responding tribes reported that they had 231 patrol cars, with an average age of 3.25 years. Of this number, 42 cars were out of service on the survey day. This information, however limited, indicates that the vehicles available to tribal officers are fairly old, and almost one out of every five is out of service on a given day.

Upon examination of the nineteen tribes that provided detailed, usable information, significant differences were obvious. There were five tribes whose reservations were both large and rural and who reported both the number of officers employed and the number of patrol vehicles. These five tribes reported having a total of 162 officers and 87 vehicles (approximately

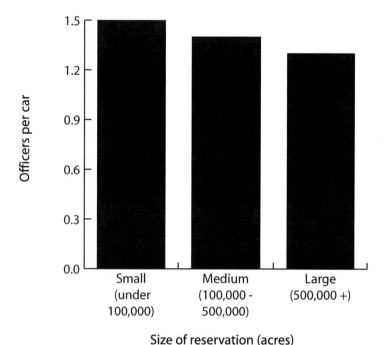

Figure 7.3. Officers per car owned by responding tribal police departments in 1996.

1.8 officers per car). On average, these vehicles were 2 years old, and 18 (or approximately 20 percent) were out of service on any given day. On the other hand, the four small, urban tribes providing detailed information reported having a total of 61 officers and 38 patrol cars (approximately 1.6 officers per car). These tribes reported that their vehicles were, on average, 3.5 years old, but only one reported that a vehicle was out of service. This makes for an interesting situation. While the police vehicles of the large rural reservations were significantly newer, they were frequently out of service, thus giving evidence of their heavy use and the potential hampering of police service. On large rural reservations, where the officers are responsible for 87 square miles per shift, officers would rely on their vehicles much more heavily than would those officers employed on a small urban reservation, where they are responsible for patrolling only 3.8 square miles.

While the federal government has addressed some aspects of the problem of patrol vehicles, it has not addressed it comprehensively. For example, one factor that must be considered regarding the availability of patrol cars is the Community Oriented Policing Services (COPS) grant program. COPS grants provide funds to support tribal police officers and to purchase equipment and patrol vehicles. While the national survey did not ask specifically for information regarding COPS-provided equipment, other studies show that COPS grants have exacerbated the issue of dysfunctional patrol vehicles.[8] Federal COPS funding is available to purchase patrol vehicles, but this funding may not be used to provide maintenance, gas, or service for vehicles. The result of this arbitrary restriction is that new or newer vehicles may sit idle at tribal police stations because the tribe is financially unable to keep them serviced and on the road.

Reflections

In 1998 a White Mountain Apache tribal police officer was killed by burglary suspects on the 1.6-million-acre Fort Apache Indian Reservation in northern Arizona. On the night he was shot, he was the only officer on duty, far from the main station or any backup.[9] This tragedy is illustrative of the problem facing so many tribal police officers every day. This death, and the deaths of so many other tribal police officers in the line of duty, must serve as a wake-up call to tribal police departments. While statistics vary, overall there are simply not enough tribal officers to do the job of policing Indian Country. And when there are not enough officers, the lives of those who are on the job are in danger.

The most obvious conclusion to be drawn from the statistics is that geographic area, 911 emergency response systems, working police radios, and availability of cover officers from surrounding agencies must be taken into consideration when evaluating the challenges facing tribal police services. Further, an adequate fleet of well-maintained and -serviced vehicles is essential if tribal officers are to be able to patrol their assigned areas.

8 Women in Tribal Policing

American Indian tribal police departments are a relatively new phenomenon.[1] As they develop they face the challenge of recruitment, hiring, and retention of responsible police personnel. A significant part of this challenge is finding recruits who can meet the qualifications set forth by the field of professional policing. While this is not a requirement for tribal police departments, which are free to hire any recruit they desire, it is a requirement for state or federal certification of these recruits. And state or federal certification is a consideration for cross-deputization with state or local law enforcement. One resource that generally meets the requirements of state certification is women.

In the non-Indian community it took many years for law enforcement agencies to begin to hire women as police officers. With men who met state certification standards readily available, the hiring of women was often a result of lawsuits filed by females who had been denied equal access. Rarely did law enforcement agencies perceive the varied skills that women bring to a job to be essential for the provision of police services. This has not been the case with tribal police departments, however, where from the beginning women have been hired as police officers.

Part of the reason tribal police departments have been open to the hiring and integration of women into law enforcement could be the fairly recent inception of tribal law enforcement, thus allowing these agencies to benefit from the changes that the field has gone through in general. Another reason could be the traditional positions of influence and authority of women in many Indian nations. These reasons, in addition to the general rule that many women were able to meet state standards, has allowed for the frequency of representation of women in tribal policing.

Given the problems of high incidence of violence, victimization, suicide, and substance abuse on reservations, it is essential that tribal police departments pursue a course that will enable them to use all available personnel to their best advantage. Low pay, high turnover, and a lack of qualified personnel hamper tribal police departments. The availability of women to fill police ranks is an opportunity that tribal police departments should not miss.

Such a course would distinguish them from non-Indian ones, where women officers are often victims of discrimination and a lack of opportunity.

During the 1996–2000 national study, 66 (38.8 percent) of the 170 tribal police departments that responded indicated that they had women in their ranks. Of these, three police departments in Washington state, two of them tribal and one immediately adjacent to a reservation, were chosen for interviews. The choices were made based on their proximity to each other, the length of time women had been in the departments, and the ranks women had achieved. In-depth, face-to-face interviews were then conducted during the summer of 2001. A total of seven members of the tribal police, both male and female and of various ranks, were interviewed regarding women within tribal policing and issues related to promotion and special assignments. The interviewees included two male police chiefs, one female detective, one male sergeant, one female and one male patrol officer, and one female reserve officer.

Women in Two Worlds

There has been little research on women tribal police officers, but research on women officers within non-Indian police departments found that one of the most serious problems is a lack of promotional opportunities.[2] Women in non-Indian police departments make up approximately 14.1 percent (or a total of approximately 76,747) of the country's 544,309 officers. Female police officers of color make up approximately 3.5 percent of the total.[3] Throughout the United States in 2000 there were approximately 1,459 tribal police officers, of which approximately 217 (14.8 percent) were women. This percentage compares favorably with the percentage of female officers in non-Indian police departments.

The comparison of female officers working in tribal custodial facilities becomes more dramatic when the percentage of women in supervisory and command ranks is considered. Women have achieved limited success in attaining higher levels of supervision and command in non-Indian police departments. Women in non-Indian police agencies hold few midlevel managerial positions (sergeant, for example) and are virtually excluded from command positions.[4] The number of women who held positions above the entry officer rank in non-Indian police departments totaled just 3.3 percent in 1986.[5]

It is here that tribal police departments markedly diverge from non-Indian police departments. The number of midlevel managerial and command positions held by women in tribal police departments is impressive. As represented by the tribes reporting pertinent information in this study, there are approximately 290 supervisory and command positions in tribal police departments. Women hold 33 (11.4 percent) of all such positions and 13 percent of the midlevel managerial positions, including twenty-four sergeant and three lieutenant positions. Further, they hold three captain and three chief positions, approximately 6.7 percent of the command positions in tribal police departments.

A strong argument for the equality that is perceived by women in tribal policing might be made when the percentage of women holding the rank of supervisor and above is compared to that of men holding such ranks. Approximately 15.2 percent of women in tribal policing hold these ranks, a rate that exceeds their representation in tribal police departments overall. Approximately 20.6 percent of men in tribal policing hold ranks of sergeant and above.

The Navajo Nation police give evidence of the strong position of women in tribal policing. This police department, the largest in Indian Country, exceeds even the respectable average held by women in tribal policing. Female tribal police officers compose approximately 21 percent of the total number of sworn officers. While women in the Navajo Nation police do well in comparison with other tribal police departments, they do even better in supervisory and command levels, where they hold more than 19 percent of the positions.

This role for women in Navajo Nation police is typified by Dorothy Laneman Fulton, who was chief of criminal investigations before becoming chief of the law enforcement department, the Navajo Nation's largest policing agency. She left Navajo Nation police to join the BIA-LES in 2003,[6] and in 2005 Ronni Wauneka was promoted to captain in the law enforcement department.[7]

While the numbers are still somewhat unbalanced, the position of women within tribal police departments is strong — significantly stronger than that of women in non-Indian police departments. This alone could account for the lack of gender-based hostility and commitment to community policing perceived by women tribal police. The empowerment of women officers to function fully as police may have a significant bearing on the ability of tribal police departments to contend successfully with the rampant violence on reservations.

The Fit of Women in Tribal Policing

Women fit well within tribal police departments. They have been hired in larger numbers and have reached positions of supervision and command more quickly and in greater numbers than in non-Indian departments. In this study, the most striking finding was the repeated emphasis on the value of women to the tribal police departments and the lack of gender-based job-related issues for women in positions of supervision and/or command.

Frequently, male tribal police chiefs spoke of their belief that tribal police departments treated women officers equally and that they were seen as equal by other officers and by the tribal communities. The chiefs repeatedly stated their commitment to the recruitment and hiring of the best personnel available. This position was underscored by the emphasis placed on the recruitment of women into police ranks and on the availability and encouragement of training opportunities.

In one tribal police department north of Seattle, a non-Indian reserve female officer was given extensive police officer training at the tribal, county, and state levels. While on the list for a full-time officer position with an adjacent, nontribal police department, she expressed her decision to stay with the tribal department — even though the pay would be significantly lower than in the other department — because tribal members and other tribal police personnel had made her feel welcome. She was enthusiastic about working in a small department that emphasized community policing, which was not generally accepted or adhered to by the non-Indian police departments with which she was familiar. She asserted that being in on the ground floor of the development of a new tribal police department gave her opportunities for training, assignment, and advancement that would not be available elsewhere. Most important, she had perceived no gender-based bias against her from either the community or her coworkers.

The chief of police, an American Indian from a different tribe than the one he serves, seconded the perceptions expressed by this female officer. He stated that, given the size of the department (a total of seven) it was essential that the members all work together in a flexible and amicable manner. He emphasized community policing, which he considered essential to working successfully on the reservation, and training that opened the eyes of officers to issues and new ways of approaching situations. He articulated the need for officers to be able to think and to evaluate situations, and his commitment to amicable resolution of community disputes.

At another tribal police department in northern Washington state, the situation for women officers was similar. A female Indian detective who is a member of a different tribe had also been recruited by non-Indian police departments but had turned down these opportunities even though the pay was significantly higher. She asserted that she had remained due to the opportunities for training and promotion and the lack of sexism she encountered on the job. She used as an example of these opportunities the fact that she had been promoted to detective within a period of five years, over many male officers with significantly longer tenure in the department.

She emphasized the flexibility of the department and its emphasis on being a good parent as well as a good officer. She stated that the department is very community oriented and that there is a lot of balance between officers of all ranks and the tribal government. She echoed University of Arizona professor Bob Thomas when she stated that "tribal police officers have roles, but they also have relationships with the community, and with each other," a situation that she contends enhances the ability of officers to work successfully at all levels.

The chief of police, an Indian from a different tribe, corroborated these perceptions. He emphasized the belief that a tribal police department should be tied to the tribal community and that the department should work with the tools they have as part of the community rather than attempting to turn a tribal police department into a state police department. He also spoke of his commitment to community policing and his belief that tribal departments should do their own felony investigations rather than turning them over to the FBI.

Such comfort levels and commitment were unfortunately not the case for one female Indian officer at an adjacent, non-Indian police department. She expressed general dissatisfaction with her department and with her situation. Three other women officers had left the department (two had left policing completely), and now she was the only female officer. She said she was not viewed as an individual but was "lumped" with other female officers deemed unsatisfactory by the department. She was the recipient of comments of a sexist nature and heard anti-Indian comments made about members of the community, although they were not directed toward her.

She frequently requested advanced training opportunities but was refused even though she had a college education and held seniority over others who were allowed to attend. She and other newer officers were trained in and committed to the concept of community policing, but the command staff and other more senior officers were not. She believed that this difference in ideology was at the heart of much of the conflict in the department.

This officer believed that her future in this department was limited. She did not feel empowered to do her best work in combating crime and violence in the community and decided that, although she was committed to law enforcement, she would leave the department.

Reflections

Women police officers experience a hostile work environment at a high rate in the non-Indian community. In a recent study, 87 percent of women police officers reported having such an experience.[8] Further studies indicate that two-thirds of 70 female officers interviewed reported at least one instance of sex discrimination, and 75 percent reported incidents of on-the-job sexual harassment.[9] The impact that such a situation can have on one's ability to do the job required of a police officer can only be imagined.

This study explored the involvement of women in tribal law enforcement and the perceptions that tribal command, fellow officers, and women tribal police themselves had of their contributions to the field. Women are highly regarded in the tribal police departments for which they work, as evidenced by the numbers of women promoted into responsible positions, and by the testimony of those with whom they work.

From the limited number of interviews conducted in this study, it would appear that women officers do not perceive tribal policing as a hostile work environment. Rather, they believe that they, their work, and their ideas are valued and that they were treated as equals. It is further evident that their male colleagues and superiors do not support the idea that tribal policing is a hostile environment for women. Rather, they emphasize the value of women as tribal police officers and the idea that when the best person for the job is selected, it might well be a woman.

The question remains whether the promotion of women to positions of responsibility influences the workplace in terms of policing styles and the perception of hostility that many women in non-Indian police departments express. It would seem that the number of women in supervisory and command positions within tribal policing may have a direct bearing on the empowerment perceived by women tribal police. The fact that a woman had recently become a tribal chief of police in the state of Washington was given by two female officers as a reason to stay within tribal policing.

An exploration of the impact of more women in supervisory and command positions could be of value. One question for additional research is to what women attribute their movement into the higher ranks of policing within a tribal context. Yet another question is whether the matrilineality or the culture and traditions of a given tribe affects the advancement of women in tribal police ranks. The traditional role of women in particular tribes and the acceptance of women in peacekeeping or other roles of influence could help to explain some of the differences for women in Indian policing, and it is these differences that make working in tribal policing so rewarding for so many women.

With the high rate of crime in tribal communities, style of policing is a serious consideration. Of significance, then, is how women in supervisory and command positions approach policing, how that approach influences those they supervise and command, how this style of policing is viewed by tribal police command, and, most important, how effective their style, whatever it might be, is in serving the community. These questions remain for additional study. But some evidence is clear. Women in tribal police departments hold positions of influence within tribal policing, and it may be their status within the field that helps reduce crime and violence in Indian Country.

9 Police Accountability in the Indian Community

Civilian oversight of police has grown and spread throughout the United States.[1] As a movement in the United States, civilian oversight of law enforcement is more than thirty years old.[2] Recent studies have determined that there are now more than ninety different civilian review procedures in the United States, and three-fourths of the fifty largest cities have some form of civilian review.[3]

Surprisingly, it now appears that civilian oversight systems are more prevalent in Indian Country than among police agencies in the non-Indian community. And, while police throughout the United States are generally opposed to civilian oversight, American Indian tribal police departments are outspoken in their support of the concept and its implementation in the communities they serve.

To date, there has been little research on tribal law enforcement or its systems of oversight. While a number of studies have been conducted of civilian oversight systems in the non-Indian community,[4] this research may not be relevant to community oversight in Indian Country.[5]

The need for assurance that policing is being conducted in an accountable and reasonable manner is as necessary for Indian Country as it is for the non-Indian community. In a study conducted by the Bureau of Indian Affairs in 1974–75, it was stated that there was an absence of police discipline in the ranks of those who provided police services to Indian Country and that both BIA and tribal police failed to maintain an adequate standard of professional conduct.[6] Officers who have been arrested and incarcerated have often been allowed to continue in their jobs, and recruiting difficulties, including low wages, have inhibited the disciplining of officers proven guilty of misconduct. Other studies have confirmed these findings.[7] Tribal police were found to have "a singularly bad reputation as being among the worst police forces in America, plagued by nepotism, poor training, high job turnover, and low pay."[8] Further, other studies found that Indian reservations in South Dakota are plagued by an "often sorry state of law enforcement."[9]

Unfortunately, tribal police misconduct continues to occur. Tribal police departments, from Ontario, Canada, to Arizona have struggled to deal with allegations of misconduct against personnel. One such series of incidents concerned a much honored tribal police officer who was suspended from a position with one Arizona tribal police department due to allegations related to previous employment with another Arizona tribal police department. He was terminated from the second department and, after leaving tribal law enforcement, was subsequently arrested in a domestic dispute.[10]

Whatever problems may exist, tribal law enforcement is an exercise of both de facto and de jure sovereignty and is essential if tribes are to provide essential services to their citizens. However, the provision of necessary services requires that the services be competent and responsible. The services need to be accountable and need to be supported by comprehensive procedures and protocols. This is particularly true with the provision of law enforcement services, where appropriate procedures and protocols to ensure the proper exercise of police authority are an essential protection for the public. Many tribes have looked to the concept of community oversight to aid them in this endeavor.

As the concept of the accountability of law enforcement becomes more prevalent, consideration must be given to the structure and implementation of such procedures in different communities. The procedures developed must be culturally sensitive and appropriate to the communities they are to serve, not just modeled after those that already exist in urban environments. Failure to do so will result in structures applicable only to an urbanized majority community.

Civilian oversight cannot be successful if it does not represent, and is not responsive to, the whole community. In urban areas, even with the best intentions, a review board may find itself under-utilized by the minority community. The problem is that many people of color feel frozen out of the inner workings of government. Although many have achieved success in the role of outsiders, and have learned how to push for change, this role may not be the most productive when dealing with the study and development of law enforcement policy and with the careful review and examination of allegations of misconduct.

Experiences that many native people who live in urban areas have with law enforcement can be problematic. The more complex problems of racism, stereotyping, and cultural norms can combine with varying levels of information regarding the propriety of specific law enforcement conduct, creating a situation where native people retreat from holding law enforcement accountable for individual acts of misconduct or for systemic failures to provide appropriate services. This failure to deal with problems can allow for their continuation. However, the problems of community oversight of tribal police are even more intricate, particularly given tribal politics, poverty, inadequate employment, inadequate education, poor housing, soaring crime rates, and other issues facing Indian communities.

Regardless of the difficulties inherent in developing and implementing community oversight of tribal police, the need to promote faith and trust in tribal law enforcement is critical. A recent study by the U.S. Department of Justice, Bureau of Justice Statistics,[11] underlines what many in the American Indian community already knew: crime victimization rates in the American Indian community are significantly higher than in the U.S. population at large, and more than twice as high as the next highest, the African American community. The rates of violent victimization for American Indian women were found to be almost 50 percent higher than that for African American men. American Indian women are also more than twice as likely to report being stalked as women of other racial or ethnic backgrounds, and approximately 70 percent of restraining orders obtained against stalkers were violated. The picture that arises from this study is that of a population victimized by persons of a different race while the perpetrator is under the influence of alcohol, and where the act of violence is much more likely to result in injuries that require medical treatment and/or hospitalization.

With this situation, it is crucial that American Indians feel comfortable and safe in contacting their police and in reporting criminal victimization. As American Indian populations strive to contend with violence, they must have confidence that their tribal police departments hold to the highest standards of policing. There must be the assurance that tribal police departments are competent guardians, free of the racism and brutality that unfortunately permeates some police departments today. Community oversight of tribal police can be a major factor in increasing community confidence in the professionalism and accountability of tribal police services.

The Legal Background

The development of tribal police is a crucial factor in the furtherance of sovereignty and self-governance.[12] Although Indian sovereignty may be a vague concept, and its parameters not clearly delineated, at its most basic it incorporates the idea of community empowerment. With the expansion of the 1975 Indian Self-Determination and Education Assistance Act (PL 638) and the Indian Self-Governance Act of 1994 (HR 4842) the stage has been set for tribes to assert their sovereignty in the area of law enforcement. It is of fundamental importance that newly created tribal law enforcement departments (particularly given their dramatic growth in recent years) include a community oversight procedure, one based in the Indian tribal community, and adhere to the highest standards of ethics and community responsiveness.

The Effect of Public Law 83-280 on Police Accountability

Public Law 83-280 is specifically discussed in chapter 11; however, I will also discuss it here as it relates to tribal police accountability. Under general principles of federal Indian law, states do not have direct jurisdiction over reservation Indians.[13] However, Congress has the power to vest federal authority with the states, which it did with the 1953 passage of PL 83-280. This has resulted in state and local police forces acting in Indian Country without being responsible to tribal councils or tribal laws.

Under PL 280, six states were delegated criminal jurisdiction over reservation Indians and civil jurisdiction over cases arising against Indians in Indian Country. Other states were permitted to assume such jurisdiction pursuant to the passage of appropriate state jurisdiction and/or state constitutional amendments. Subsequent to the passage of this legislation ten states accepted such jurisdiction.

PL 280 established state jurisdiction without abolishing tribal jurisdiction. The tribes in these states often have police departments even though under PL 280 the states are required to provide law enforcement services. In these instances, and in others, tribal and state powers are concurrent even though some states, particularly California, have denied that such tribal jurisdiction exists.[14] Specifically, PL 280 gives the named states the same power to enforce their regular criminal laws inside Indian Country that they have always exercised outside of it. There is no requirement that the state or local police departments be accountable to the tribes they serve.

While federal law enforcement agencies have jurisdiction throughout Indian Country, there currently is no civilian oversight system with jurisdiction over misconduct by federal law enforcement, including the FBI.[15] This limits the ability of tribes to deal effectively with misconduct allegations made against federal law enforcement.

The Structures and Function of Civilian Oversight Systems

There are five basic classifications of civilian oversight systems.[16] These classifications include Class IA and IB, where individual citizen complaints are received and investigated by persons who are not sworn police officers. Class IA procedures require that a board that makes recommendations to the police executive review the investigative reports. These recommendations are advisory only, and the boards do not have the authority to hire or fire. Class IB procedures are headed by an executive director who sends recommendations to the police executive. There is no board in this structure.

In Class II systems, citizen complaints are investigated internally by sworn police officers. The report of the investigation is then forwarded to a civilian oversight system, either a board or a single person, who reviews the report and makes recommendations to the police executive. In Class III systems, citizen complaints are investigated and disposed by the police department. There is an appellate procedure that allows a civilian oversight system to review the complaint disposition upon request of the complainant. Finally, Class IV systems include an auditor component. The complaint is investigated and disposed by the police department. The auditor monitors the operations of the complaint process but is not involved in individual complaints.

While civilian oversight systems have been in place in American cities for many years, there have been few scientific studies of their long-term effectiveness in making substantive improvements in the police departments over which they have jurisdiction. A research brief published by the Open Society Institute Center on Crime, Communities, and Culture notes that while civilian oversight systems have proliferated in cities in response to incidents of police misconduct, there is only limited evidence of their success in controlling such incidents. However, this report concludes that the results experienced by municipal civilian oversight systems provide for "cautious optimism."[17]

Additional studies have come to the conclusion that external oversight of law enforcement can be an essential part of effective police accountability.[18] Though the scientific studies are few and most information regarding effectiveness is anecdotal, the cities cited above and others have undertaken and/or strengthened civilian oversight of their law enforcement agencies.

Any of the classes of oversight systems can prove to be effective. All establish the principle of police accountability, serve as sources for information about police misconduct, and act as early warning systems for police administrators. In addition, they serve to empower communities. They give voice to the proper concerns of the citizens of the community and create procedures to ensure that these concerns are heard.

Community Oversight in Indian Country

Given the recent growth in American Indian Tribal Police Departments, the opportunity now exists to look at the development and implementation of police accountability systems in Indian Country.[19] In the 1996–2000 surveys, forty-nine tribes provided usable information regarding this component, with twenty-five departments responding that they had a formal procedure for handling complaints against police personnel. Follow-up telephone interviews of tribal police chiefs or administrative staff were completed with twenty-two of these twenty-five departments, with three interviews unable to be completed with appropriate personnel.

The interviews consisted of questions regarding the composition and structure of the oversight systems, the date when the system was established, how members were selected, and whether there were members representing law enforcement or with law enforcement experience. The interview questions asked about whether there were any public hearing components of the systems and whether police personnel records were held confidential. The jurisdiction of the system was determined with respect to whether the powers of the system were advisory or mandatory, whether there were any constraints as to what types of allegations could be reviewed, and whether the system had the authority to review and recommend policy. The interviewees were questioned regarding the general feelings of law enforcement about the system and in particular about any specific concerns that had been expressed. The questions were asked in an open-ended manner, with follow-up questions asked as necessary.

Findings of the Study

The need for formal community oversight systems has been recognized by a significant number of American Indian tribes. It is of particular note that while civilian oversight systems in the majority community have grown in number over the last thirty years, they still represent a small percentage of all police departments in the United States. In contrast, community oversight components were part of the police complaint procedure of twenty-five of the forty-nine American Indian tribal police departments that responded to this question.

Community oversight in Indian Country is not a new phenomenon. While many oversight systems were formed after the departments were implemented, the majority have been in existence since the creation of the tribal police departments.[20]

The Structure of Community Oversight Systems
Community oversight in Indian Country incorporates components of civilian oversight found in the non-Indian community. Fourteen of the twenty-

Table 9.1   Structure of Tribal Police Oversight Boards

Tribe	Composition of board	Officers on board	Jurisdiction	Authority	Policy	Public meetings	Confidentiality of records
Santa Ana	Tribal council	Yes (1)	Anything	Mandatory	Yes	Yes	—
Rocky Boy's	Tribal council/ law enforcement committee	No	Anything	Advisory	Yes	Yes	—
Pine Ridge	Independent	No	Anything	De facto advisory	Yes	Yes	Yes
Lac du Flambeau	Independent	No	Anything	Mandatory	Yes	Yes	Yes
Spirit Lake	Independent	Yes	Anything	Advisory	Yes	Yes	Yes
Menominee	Independent	No	Anything	Advisory	Yes	Yes	Yes
White River	Independent	Yes (balanced)	Anything	Advisory	Yes	Yes	Yes
San Carlos	Tribal council/ law enforcement committee	No	Anything	Advisory	Yes	Yes	—
Muckleshoot	Independent	No	Anything	Mandatory	Yes	Yes	Yes
Fort Hall	Independent	Yes	Anything	Advisory	Yes	Yes	Yes
Kickapoo	Independent	Yes (balanced)	Anything	Mandatory	No	Yes	Yes
Cheyenne Arapaho	Independent, elected	Yes	Anything	Mandatory	No	No	Yes
Saint Regis Mohawk	Independent	No	Appellate	Advisory	No	Yes (upon request)	Yes
Creek	Independent, elected	No	Anything	Advisory	Yes	Yes	Yes
Navajo	Tribal council	Yes	Anything	Advisory	Yes	Yes	Yes
Rosebud	Independent, appointed	Yes	Anything	Advisory	No	Yes	Yes
Lummi	Independent, appointed	Yes	Anything	Advisory	Yes	Yes	Yes
Mohegan	Ombudsman	Yes	Anything	Advisory	Yes	Yes	Yes
Hannaville	Independent/ Tribal council	No	Anything	Advisory	Yes	No	No
Fort Peck	Independent	Yes	Intake	Advisory	No	No	Yes
Omaha	Ombudsman	Yes	Anything	Advisory	Yes	Yes	Yes
Cheyenne River	Independent/ tribal council	Yes	Anything	Advisory	Yes	Yes	Yes

two tribal systems consist of an elected or appointed board, independent from either the tribal council or the tribal police department.[21] Two tribal systems consist of an independent auditor/ombudsman with independent authority over the police complaint process,[22] and others consist of tribal council subcommittees that have authority over law enforcement (see table 9.1).[23]

Although an in-depth analysis of Indian Country police oversight systems has yet to be done, the initial survey of these systems indicates that they are generally following the classifications established in the previous section. Every tribal oversight system contacted for this study was either a Class II, Class III, or Class IV procedure. Complaints are received by either the tribal police departments or the oversight systems, and in most cases either one is acceptable. However, in one tribe the community oversight system is designated specifically to do the intake of complaints.[24] The initial investigation of citizen complaints in those tribal communities studied was done by law enforcement, although in some instances of serious allegations of misconduct the investigation is conducted by a geographically adjacent or federal agency.

Jurisdiction

The jurisdiction of the tribal community oversight systems is generally very broad. Seventy-five percent had policy authority. This in itself is striking. Policy authority is the ability to examine the policies and procedures of the police department and to make recommendations for new policies. Many experts view policy authority as an extremely important component for law enforcement oversight systems.[25] Review of police policy is a proactive approach that serves to improve policing and prevent problems before they occur.

More than 85 percent of tribal systems may look at any allegation of misconduct they choose. More than 75 percent of the systems were advisory to the tribal police chief, with the rest having mandatory authority. In some cases, however, the recommendations by systems with advisory powers were treated as mandatory by the tribal police department, something that has not occurred in civilian oversight mechanisms generally.[26]

One tribal government has specifically addressed the problem of accountability of surrounding local law enforcement. This tribe, in a PL 280 state, recently contracted with a county sheriff's department and a city police department to provide law enforcement services to the reservation. A specific provision of the contract was the creation of a tribal community oversight system with authority to participate in the selection of officers employed by the county and city agencies to serve on the reservation. The tribal oversight committee also will participate in the complaint process for the city police selected for reservation service, and any disciplinary recommendations made by this committee will be mandatory on the employing agency.[27]

The Role of Law Enforcement

Tribal communities generally were not reluctant to include law enforcement in their oversight systems. Although at the time few boards actually had law enforcement members, many had had them at one time. Some structures required that law enforcement be represented on the community oversight board.[28]

Including law enforcement representatives on the community oversight board as full voting members raises the issue of independence. Oversight systems generally are constructed to bring a nonpolice viewpoint to the analysis of the propriety of police conduct. This viewpoint is then juxtaposed with that of the police when the disposition of the case is rendered. To involve police personnel in both the community analysis and fact-finding phases as well as in the disposition phase may dilute the community analysis of the issue and call the independence of the process into question.

Board Membership

While most tribes require that the members of oversight boards both be tribal members and reside on the reservation, some boards have tribal members who do not live on the reservation.[29] One tribe designates a position on the community oversight board for someone who resides in an adjacent community and is not a tribal member.[30]

Confidentiality

All of the tribal oversight systems consider police personnel records confidential. In some instances, members of the community oversight system may view the records, but this is rare. Meetings held by the community oversight boards are generally public, although not always. In three tribes the meetings are confidential,[31] and in one tribe the meeting may be public upon request of the subject officer.[32]

Tribal Police Response

The tribal police contacted were overwhelmingly supportive of community oversight. This is in stark contrast with the common experience in the non-Indian community, in which "police officers bitterly oppose civilian review." Observations by police interviewed included the comments that the oversight system was "protection for the public" and "we all know each other; we're all related clanwise."[33]

Other researchers have substantiated the opinions police in this study expressed in support of community oversight. One study of a Great Plains tribal police department observed that "none of the distrust and rancor typical of relations between police and civilian oversight commissions else-where was in evidence."[34] That study further found that tribal police viewed the community oversight system as helpful in accomplishing the profession-alism that the police department wanted to achieve. It is this feeling of community connection that exemplifies the best of tribal policing and helps ease the way for community oversight to function.

This is not to say that no problems with the community oversight sys-tems were perceived by tribal law enforcement. Four of the twenty-two po-lice personnel interviewed noted some concerns with how the community oversight systems operated. These concerns included a lack of experience among oversight system members, the effects of nepotism on system deci-sions, questions of conflict of interest, and a feeling that the participants in the oversight system either were adversarial with the police department or did not undertake sufficient advocacy on their behalf. However, these con-cerns did not outweigh the support given by police administrators to the concept of community oversight even in those instances where problems were reported.

Reflections

The development of community oversight systems in Indian Country is an opportunity for a deeper analysis of the civilian oversight movement. To date there has been little research into which civilian oversight system works best and why some fail after a few years. Usually failure is attributed to budgetary constraints, a weak investigative staff, or a general failure of the political will.[35] The study of such systems in Indian Country may help to clarify why these systems are generally viewed as successful and are sup-ported by tribal law enforcement.

Some reasons for the success of tribal community oversight systems may be the fact that most were created concurrently with the formation of the tribal police departments. This integration of the system with the department from the beginning may help to create an effective working relationship and ease the concerns that can result when an oversight system comes about as a result of particular problems or issues. One tribal police administrator cred-ited the police support of community oversight to the department's commit-ment to community policing. He stated that there were issues between "tra-ditional" members (meaning those officers who participated in traditional cultural activities) and "professional" members of the department. He as-serted that these differences were smoothed out by the integration of the police and the community.

Another possible reason for the perceived success of tribal community oversight may be the ability of most systems to deal with law enforcement policy rather than simply reacting to allegations of misconduct. The inability to deal with law enforcement policy has been seen as a major weakness of civilian oversight systems in the non-Indian community.[36]

However, for community oversight to be fully successful, it is necessary to address the concerns voiced by tribal police administrators. It is of primary importance that decisions of the boards be viewed as fair and impartial. Any decision that seems to be influenced by nepotism will significantly erode the trust that law enforcement and members of the community have in the community oversight process. Board members' conflicts of interest are also of great concern. As with concerns about nepotism, board members need to be viewed as fair and impartial for their reviews and decisions to be given full weight.

It is the job of those of us who value good policing and the concept of police accountability to consider ways in which the idea of civilian oversight can fit different peoples with differing worldviews. The need to work with police agencies to reduce the frequency of misconduct complaints and to hold individual officers accountable is critical if we are to improve police service for everyone.

While there are many avenues to and methods of accomplishing effective oversight of law enforcement, the experiences of Indian Country have much to offer the field. The development and implementation of tribal community oversight systems may illustrate how significant the establishment of early warning systems is on the retention of police officers. Early warning systems allow police administrations to intercede before patterns of misconduct become established, thus causing officers to be retrained or counseled at an early stage of improper behavior rather than being dismissed as a result of egregious misconduct. The implementation of such procedures in Indian Country will increase knowledge of the importance of such monitoring throughout the field of policing.

Investigation of complaints is a point of contention in the non-Indian community. Generally, civilian oversight systems in which investigators external to the police department conduct the investigations are considered more independent.[37] Thus, the creation of community oversight systems in which police officers conduct all investigations should be examined for the adequacy and impartiality of investigations, as well as for community support of dispositions.

Further examination is needed of the extent of tribal community support for tribal police and for the sufficiency of the mechanisms for discipline and control. While this exploratory study has scratched the surface of tribal community oversight, further research could help determine how integrated tribal police are with the communities they serve and how accountable the communities believe the police departments should be to the public. Given the information obtained in this study, the need for additional research is apparent, particularly with regard to how the concept of civilian oversight should be enhanced in Indian Country. The following are some specific recommendations for future study:

- The process of the development and implementation of tribal police departments should be examined, particularly as to whether the concurrent implementation of community oversight systems results in greater acceptance of the concept by members of the police departments.
- The devolution of power to, and community consultation with, a broad-based circle of responsible leaders is a common approach to decision making in many Indian communities. Research should be conducted as to whether the acceptance of community oversight and the role of tribal members in the formulation of policy is affected by a tribal police department's strong community-oriented policing approach or by significant training from mainstream police agencies.
- Tribal governments and police departments should develop codes, ordinances, and police protocols that clearly spell out proper conduct in given situations. One criticism often levied against tribal police systems is a lack of fully developed police protocols. Where such protocols exist, research should be conducted regarding whether the community oversight system supports holding officers accountable for their violations and whether such accountability reduces repetition of misconduct.
- There should be an examination of whether holding public meetings on police misconduct, policy development, or failures have an effect on public support for tribal police.

Through additional research into community oversight in Indian Country, it may be possible to help strengthen and empower tribal governments, improve tribal policing, and give voice to members of tribal communities. What could be learned from such research could also help to develop civilian oversight structures that facilitate the participation of all segments of communities throughout the United States, be they tribal, rural, or urban.

10 Tribal Jails and Corrections

Jails in Indian Country are a long-standing concern.[1] Like other aspects of tribal policing, Indian detention facilities, whether run by the Bureau of Indian Affairs or by tribal governments, have been the subject of recent studies. The U.S. Department of the Interior, Office of the Inspector General, issued a study in September 2004 entitled "Neither Safe nor Secure: An Assessment of Indian Detention Facilities." This study found that jails managed and overseen by tribal chiefs of police were more efficiently operated and managed than BIA-operated jails.[2]

The incarceration rate for American Indians, noted in a 1999 Bureau of Justice Statistics study, is startling. The study found that American Indians were held in local jails at the highest rate of any racial group. Another study was published by the BJS in July 2000.[3] This study found that the number of American Indians incarcerated throughout the United States was 19,679 on June 30, 1999.[4] Further, on a per capita basis, American Indians were incarcerated in prisons at a rate that was 38 percent higher than the national rate. The September 2004 Bureau of the Interior study focuses on the conditions present in Indian Country jails. It does not have specific statistics regarding criminality in Indian Country.

The predominant factor found in the 1999 BJS study was the effect of alcohol consumption. Almost half (46 percent) of all convicted American Indians in local jails had been under the influence of alcohol when they committed the offense for which they had been convicted. This percentage rises to 70 percent when only violent crimes are considered.[5] This rate is in stark contrast with all other racial groups, where only a third or fewer of the convicted non-Indians were reported to be under the influence of alcohol during the commission of nonviolent crimes, and 41 percent for violent crimes. This high incidence of substance abuse is no longer generally addressed in non-Indian prisons and jails. Thus, Indian people held in non-Indian facilities often do not have access to programs that might assist them in avoiding substance abuse on the outside. This is not the case in jails in Indian Country, where 59 of 69 facilities offered substance abuse programs, and 57 of the 69 offered counseling and education programs.[6]

The crime rates in Indian Country create a demand for incarceration and corrections systems that reduce crime. The incarceration of American Indians takes place in various types of facilities. Federal prisons are the place of incarceration for American Indians accused of enumerated felonies covered by the Major Crimes Act passed in 1885.[7] Facilities run by the Bureau of Indian Affairs are also prevalent in Indian Country. In other instances, particularly in those states covered under Public Law 280, which became law in 1953, American Indians are held in state jails and prison systems.[8] In many other cases, tribal jails are the place of incarceration.

The conditions revealed in these statistics, and the environment they create in Indian Country, are problems for both tribal governments and tribal law enforcement agencies. Building and maintaining jails is expensive, as is implementing corrections systems that reduce recidivism and help to heal communities, but the human cost of not doing so is even more expensive.

The sovereignty of Indian nations is a concept that can be advanced in legal and/or de facto manner. Establishing tribal government structures and institutions and extending tribal jurisdiction, where appropriate, are efforts that expand tribal sovereignty while meeting the needs of tribal members. Establishment and implementing tribal jails is one such effort, but it does not come without cost. Making decisions, developing policies and protocols, and recruiting and training staff are problems that have to be overcome if crime and criminality are to ease in Indian Country. It is these challenges that are the focus of this chapter.

Tribal Jails

The 2000 BJS study of Indian detention facilities found that sixty-nine jails, affiliated with fifty-three tribes, were operating in Indian Country. These jails were located in eighteen states, some of them PL 280 states. The jails are run by various agencies, with forty-eight run by Indian Nations, twenty run by the BIA, and one run privately. Tribal consortiums jointly run four of the jails, while a number of the others receive inmates from other tribes on a contract basis. BIA data reported in the study indicated that tribal jails employed 659 persons and had an authorized inmate capacity of approximately 2,100 adults and juveniles. In 1999 the actual jail population in Indian Country was almost 1,700.[9]

The September 2004 Bureau of the Interior study found that, while there had been a growth in detention facilities in Indian Country (to seventy-two), the problems remained. The jails, including the newest, are generally overcrowded. More than half (53 percent) reportedly were "habitually over-crowded," with inmates often sleeping on the floor.[10] Seventy-nine percent of the facilities were found to be below minimum staffing levels on a regular basis.[11] The physical condition of the majority of the inspected jails was "abysmal — the result of years of neglect and failure to perform even routine repairs in a timely manner," and even those jails that were relatively new (less than four years old) were already deteriorating.[12]

Although the BIA has received millions of dollars in federal funding (e.g., $10 million allocated for 1999 to 2001 to hire 305 additional detention officers), much of this money has not been spent for the stated purpose. Further, there was little or no accountability for the expended funds. The Department of Justice provided more than $150 million in construction grants to build new jails. Of the thirteen new jails scheduled to be completed by April 2004, only two are open and occupied. Nine are completed but not operational due to a lack of staff, and two remain uncompleted.[13] The 2004 report concludes with the following: "The BIA is sitting on a liability time bomb and must act to diffuse it now so that modest funds available can be used for their intended purpose, instead of potentially being consumed by legal fees, fines, and judgments."[14]

Regulatory Rules and Laws

American Indian nations are sovereign. They operate under their own laws and rules and have jurisdiction over their own members and Indians of other tribes. Absent PL 280, American Indian nations are not subject to the laws of the states in which they are located. Further, American Indian nations retain sovereign immunity and may not be sued.[15] However, the operation of tribal jails is subject to the Indian Civil Rights Act of 1968 (ICRA),[16] which provides that no Indian nation exercising self-government shall deny any of its citizens certain rights, among them the right to be free from excessive bond or cruel and unusual punishment. Further, where the wording of ICRA is similar to or identical to the wording of the U.S. Constitution, the courts have found that the language in ICRA may be given the interpretation given the Constitution.[17]

Under this analysis, the jails of American Indian nations can be held to standards set by the Eighth Amendment of the U.S. Constitution. The Eighth Amendment prohibits confinement of convicted prisoners under sub-standard conditions that involve unnecessary and wanton infliction of pain.[18] Prisoners must be provided with reasonably adequate food, clothing, shelter, sanitation, medical care, and personal safety.[19] They must be confined in an environment that does not result in their degeneration or that threatens their mental and physical well-being,[20] and that meets standards that are not "incompatible with the evolving standards of decency that mark the progress of a maturing society."[21]

The issue of overcrowding is yet another instance in which the Eighth Amendment may be violated. The courts have held that whether overcrowding of a jail violates the Eighth Amendment depends on the length of time prisoners are held in overcrowded conditions, the level of overcrowding, and whether overcrowding affects sanitation or medical care.[22]

Compliance with Federal Guidelines

Federal guidelines for the operation of jails and prisons are extensive, but they do not necessarily cover tribal jails. Many tribal jails operate under the 1975 Indian Self-Determination and Education Assistance Act, and the resulting "638 contract."[23] Under this contract, the American Indian nation agrees to meet Bureau of Indian Affairs standards. Further, where tribal police are employed pursuant to a 638 contract, they are designated by the Bureau of Indian Affairs to carry out the federal government's responsibilities.

The Bureau of Indian Affairs has formulated minimum standards for detention programs on Indian reservations that are included in Chapter 1, Bureau of Indian Affairs, Part 11: Law and Order on Indian Reservations, Subpart C: Criminal Procedure. These standards include guidelines for medical care, safety of inmates, and numbers of inmates allowed in each cell.[24] However, even though these standards are established, the conditions that exist within tribal jails are frequently in violation.

The Cost of Running a Tribal Jail

The cost of running a tribal jail is a significant commitment by any law enforcement agency, particularly one with limited resources. Most tribal police departments run on extremely limited budgets. Almost half of all tribal police agencies (46.6 percent) have operating budgets of $500,000 or less. These budgets comprise a bundle of funding. For almost half of the tribal police departments (41.4 percent), the Bureau of Indian Affairs provides 100 percent of the funding. Only 17.2 percent indicate that they receive none of their budget from the BIA. However the departments are funded, the expenditures for incarceration and corrections are a heavy commitment. The question is whether these expenditures bring a level of value to tribal communities that makes the outlay of funds worthwhile.

Staffing Tribal Jails

Tribal jails exist throughout Indian Country. The jails are generally small and employ staff in numbers out of proportion to the rest of tribal law enforcement. The ten largest jails house approximately 40 percent of those in custody in Indian Country. These ten largest jails are all in Arizona, with Gila River's Sacaton Juvenile Detention Facility having a rated capacity of 100 and the Sacaton Adult Detention Facility having a capacity of 86. With their third detention facility, the Gila River facilities have the capacity to house 230 inmates, making this the largest in Indian Country. The Tohono O'odham Detention Center, while rated for 33 adults and 16 juveniles, housed a total of 98 inmates at midyear in 1999. The eight facilities of the Navajo Nation have a total capacity of 206 detainees. On the other end of the spectrum, forty-two of the sixty-nine tribal jails (61 percent) are rated for fewer than 25 inmates, and nineteen of the sixty-nine (27 percent) are rated for fewer than 10 inmates.[25]

For many tribes, staffing a jail is a serious commitment. According to the

Table 10.1   Staffing of Tribal Jails and Law Enforcement Departments

Tribe	Police staff		Jail staff	
	Male	Female	Male	Female
Colorado River Indian Tribes	30	2	9	12
Navajo	231	61	40	51
Pascua Yaqui	18	3	11	9
San Carlos	20	0	11	9
White Mountain Apache	41	10	4	9
Blackfeet	23	1	1	7
Flathead	17	1	2	4
Fort Peck	19	2	5	7
Northern Cheyenne	9	1	2	3
Rocky Boy	5	0	4	5
Omaha	7	0	2	5
Jicarilla	22	5	7	5
Pine Ridge	101	10	5	8
Sisseton-Wahpeton	10	6	6	2
Puyallup	16	2	4	4
Yakima	30	2	5	5
Menominee	29	4	10	7

2000 BJS study, sixty-six of the sixty-nine facilities studied asserted that they needed additional jail staff to meet the needs of running the jail, and sixty-seven reported that their staff needed additional training. Most tribal police departments are relatively small. For some of these, the staff assigned to run and maintain jail services can adversely affect police services available to the whole tribal community. The jail staffing numbers referenced in table 10.1 include only those personnel actually assigned to guard functions. The numbers do not include administration or facilities personnel, which in many instances would increase the numbers significantly.

The Incarceration of Juveniles in Indian Country

Indian people have had many adverse experiences in jails and prisons run by federal, state, and local governments. These experiences are complicated by the age of the detainees. The number of American Indian youths in custody is on the rise. A recent study by the Bureau of Justice Statistics found that the number increased 50 percent between 1994 and 2000.[26] Throughout Indian Country, juveniles account for 16 percent of the total number of people in custody. Federal guidelines require that juveniles be kept out of view or hearing of adult prisoners; however, not all tribal jails comply with such rules. Of the forty-three facilities eligible to hold juveniles, in nine jails juveniles were separated from adults by sight only (21 percent), and in four facilities (9 percent) juveniles were not separated from adults at all.

The federal government does not own or operate any juvenile detention facilities. Thus, requirements enacted for the safety of juveniles can complicate the situation for youth in temporary custody for substance abuse. Ted Quasula, director of BIA Law Enforcement Services, has been quoted as saying, "It's not uncommon for a juvenile to ride around in the back of a squad car until they sober up somewhat, because we simply don't have the facilities."[27] The lack of federal juvenile detention facilities requires that American Indian youth under federal supervision be incarcerated in public and private jail facilities far from their home communities, thus increasing their alienation from their culture and kinship relations.[28]

Tribal jails have tried to address these problems by developing tribal juvenile facilities. Eight facilities deal specifically with the incarceration of juveniles, and two of them are run by the Navajo Nation. While tribal jails that house adults routinely exceed their rated capacity, that is not the case with these juvenile facilities. On June 30, 1999, tribal jails housed 197 male juvenile inmates and 70 female inmates, and only one juvenile facility exceeded its rated capacity.[29]

The Tribal Incarceration of Adults

The situation for American Indian youth is echoed in the adult Indian community, with adults subjected to difficult experiences and cultural dislocation by incarceration within the non-Indian world. Thus, while developing and staffing tribal jails can be both a financial and an operational burden for tribes, they can also bring significant benefits for tribal people. Allowing tribal members to be housed within or close to their home tribal community, thus increasing the possibility of family and cultural contacts while also holding miscreants directly accountable to the Indian nations themselves, can be a significant step forward for law and order in Indian Country.

Inmates in tribal jails are generally those convicted of misdemeanors. Ten facilities held inmates convicted of felonies, and nine held only those inmates in detention for less than seventy-two hours.[30] Tribal jails are routinely overcrowded, with eleven in 1999 under a court order or consent decree that restricted the maximum number of inmates who could be incarcerated.

On June 30, 1999, tribal jails housed 1,354 male inmates and 223 female inmates. More than half of the adult detention facilities operated above 100 percent capacity, and fifteen (22 percent) operated at above 150 percent of rated capacity. Approximately 5 percent of inmates in tribal jails were housed in areas not originally intended for holding prisoners. Eleven percent of inmates in tribal jails were double-bunked in single-occupancy cells, and 7 percent of inmates were housed in holding areas or drunk tanks.[31]

Overcrowding in smaller facilities was worse than in larger ones. In mid-1999, Indian Country jails were at 108 percent capacity, while the occupancy rate for jails with capacities of fewer than ten was 161 percent of capacity, and 155 percent of capacity for those rated to hold up to twenty-four inmates.

Case Study Examples

During the course of my research in 2000–2001, site visits and interviews were conducted at three tribes. Two tribes, the Tohono O'odham and the Puyallup, operate tribal jails. The Tohono O'odham house only their own prisoners, though on occasion they provide a holding space for federal detainees. The Puyallup tribe has a regional jail with contractual relationships with a number of tribes in the Pacific Northwest. The third, the Lummi Nation, does not have its own jail but instead has a contract with the county within which the tribe is located. I interviewed the chiefs of police and jail personnel of the Puyallup and Tohono O'odham. I also interviewed the jail director for Whatcom County in regard to Lummi prisoners.

The Tohono O'odham

The primary issue for the Tohono O'odham jail is severe overcrowding. The jail is rated to hold 33 adult prisoners, but according to jail administrators, this number has often exceeded 130. Due to transportation issues and the costs attendant to housing prisoners pursuant to a contract, the nation does not transport or house any inmates in facilities of another Indian nation, the BIA, or the county. Due to overcrowding, there is minimal movement within the jail and limited access to diversion programs, advocacy services, or ceremonies. All of the inmates are members of the O'odham community. The nation does not contract with other Indian nations to house their prisoners, as there are not enough beds.

In 1995 the BIA and the U.S. Department of Justice, National Institute of Corrections, conducted a facility review and preliminary assessment of the Tohono O'odham detention facility that had been requested by the support services commander of the Tohono O'odham Nation police department.[32] The review found that there were many facility-related problems, including inefficient design, malfunctioning mechanical systems, and overcrowding. The report further found that overcrowding, inadequate staffing, a lack of written policies and procedures, and a lack of space for effective programs resulted in a number of operational deficiencies. Six years later, the site visit confirmed that these problems continued, although they were being addressed.

The O'odham jail is supported solely through tribal funding. In the past, the nation received funding for the jail from the Bureau of Indian Affairs. Now, due to the overcrowded conditions, federal funding has been largely eliminated, leaving the nation to support the jail mainly through tribal funding. The jail costs $1.2 million per year to operate, of which $300,000 comes from BIA 638 funding. The nation applied recently for grant funding, but it was denied because it is a gaming tribe, placing it very low on the priority list. Other grant proposals are now in process.

The overcrowded conditions are complicated by a number of situations. For example, while the average stay is ten to fifteen days, one inmate is serving a sentence of twelve years. One cell is used for suicide watch and is absolutely bare. It is supposed to be used for minimal periods of time, but due to the overcrowded conditions, individual inmates have remained there for ten to fifteen days at a time. The drunk tank is yet another feature impacted by overcrowding. It now contains double bunks but has no bathroom or television. It has been used to house up to ten inmates at a time.

Yet another issue was overcrowding due to tribal police and U.S. Border Patrol personnel picking up undocumented aliens on tribal land. The traditional lands of the nation are split by a seventy-five-mile stretch of the U.S.–Mexico border. Frequently, tribal police and Border Patrol agents apprehend migrants crossing the border illegally. Until 2004, these migrants were transported to the jail and held there until the U.S. Border Patrol transported them to a federal facility in Tucson. This practice resulted in scores of migrants being held in the yard of the jail for up to six hours. The nation provided water and food for these people, who on some occasions exceeded 300. The nation was not compensated for the provision of custodial service, food, or water, and the jail staff had to ensure that the detainees were safe and sheltered.

This practice was a problem for jail personnel, as well as for the inmates. The detainees were placed in the jail yard, the sole recreation area for inmates and also the location of the classroom, where all education, counseling, and programs are held. Advocate services are also conducted in the classroom, as are church services and meetings between inmates and their families.

The nation decided that the situation was no longer tenable and stopped holding detainees for the U.S. Border Patrol. The nation also improved the staffing and upkeep of the facility, and placed more than 100 bunks in the cells. Now only a limited number of inmates sleep on the floor. In addition, a multimillion-dollar grant was obtained recently to build a new minimum-security facility.

The nation has also made an effort to incorporate traditional ceremonies, which are considered a privilege at the Tohono O'odham jail. An average of fifteen to twenty inmates wish to participate in traditional ceremonies, and their participation depends upon good behavior and a process of random selection from among those who request to participate. Traditional healers meet with inmates in the yard and a sweathouse. Some believe there is a need for more spiritual healing, and traditional elders have come to the jail to work with individual inmates. Although the nation is largely Roman Catholic, church services are also limited.

The 2004 Bureau of the Interior study of tribal jails found that the Tohono O'odham detention facility was exceptional in a number of ways. Unlike many other tribal jails, the Tohono O'odham facility had a field training officer (FTO) program to enhance the skills of newly hired custodial personnel. It also had an FTO manual with established policies and procedures, and jail administrators had experience and formal training from working in other detention programs.[33] While the Tohono O'odham jail facility had maintenance problems and staff shortages, the tribes had made program improvements and achieved meaningful results.[34]

The Puyallup

Unlike the Tohono O'odham, the Puyallup nation maintains a regional jail for the tribes of the Pacific Northwest. The jail has a bed capacity of twenty-five, with an average jail population of ten to fifteen. The highest number of inmates was twenty-three. With this low average jail population, the Puyallup nation has been able to enter into contracts with a number of the twelve tribes in the I-5 corridor. At present, seven of the twelve tribes have contracts with the Puyallup to house their prisoners.

The Puyallup jail houses only native prisoners. Approximately 40 percent of the inmates are Puyallup tribal members. The jail admits only misdemeanor offenders with a maximum sentence of one year. The average stay is from seven to thirty days. The jail requires inmates to serve time certain — that is, a specific amount of time without possibility of early parole — and absent a tribal court order, does not allow for early release. Since 1977 the nation has not housed juveniles, due to issues regarding "sight and sound separation." Currently there is a move to build a juvenile facility.

The jail has recently undergone a complete remodeling to bring it up to federal codes. The cost to complete this upgrading was $350,000. The operational cost is approximately $300,000 per year. The costs are primarily borne by the Puyallup Nation, with some federal funding. Additional funding is received from contracts with other tribes to house their prisoners.

The primary issue for the jail, besides meeting federal requirements, has been staffing. The jail operates in a Public Law 280 state. All jail staff members are state certified and cross-deputized with the state of Washington and with the county. Seventy percent of the staff is native, with half of those being Puyallup tribal members. Four of the eight staff members are female, as is the chief jailer. The chief of police favors the hiring of female staff because he believes individual inmates open up to female staff in a way that they would not to male staff.

The training level of the staff is very high. The Puyallup Nation emphasizes professional staff development, with internal and federal training as well as participation in state training programs. The jail staff also conducts training sessions for the staff of surrounding agencies. The fact that staff is highly qualified results in a high attrition rate, however, as custodial staff frequently leave for other jurisdictions, where salaries are significantly higher.

The Lummi

The Lummi tribe is located in Whatcom County, Washington. Washington is a PL 280 state, and thus all enumerated major crimes are under state jurisdiction. The Lummi have asserted tribal jurisdiction over all misdemeanors committed by Indians on the reservation and over all juvenile crimes other than homicide. The tribe has its own police department and judicial system but does not maintain its own jail. Rather, the tribe maintains contracts with Whatcom County to house both adult and juvenile tribal prisoners.

The contract is negotiated for two years at a time. The 2000 contract was per bed night, with a charge of $90 per night for juveniles and $53 for adults. The total cost for 2000 was $60,000 for adults and $13,000 for juveniles. In addition, the tribe is billed separately for any necessary medical services for tribal inmates. Additionally, the Lummi tribal court handles the prosecution of all charges. While a defense attorney is not required under the Indian Civil Rights Act, the tribal attorney has required that the tribe provide a defense attorney for all criminal charges.

This incarceration arrangement seems to meet the needs of the Lummi tribe, and they report no problems between tribal prisoners and jail personnel. When the Lummi tribe decided that it wanted inmates to serve time certain rather than being allowed to earn early release, the county agreed even though this was contrary to county laws. Another issue was the length of time tribal detainees were incarcerated pending arraignment. Lengthy stays prior to arraignment by tribal courts were a problem for the county jail. As a result of negotiations between the county and the tribe, the tribal court now holds a probable cause hearing within forty-eight hours of arrest.

The issue of access to ceremonies and religious activities has been resolved through agreement. There is no place for ceremonies in the Whatcom County Jail. Instead, when ceremonies are to be held the tribal court issues temporary releases, and the county releases the prisoners into tribal custody. The prisoner is escorted to the ceremony by tribal personnel and then returned to county custody.

In the past, the county had limited beds for juveniles, so youths sentenced to detention by the Lummi tribal court were denied entry. The tribe then contracted for a designated bed at the county juvenile facility for tribal youth. However, elders have begun to intercede with minor criminal conduct by juveniles. The tribal court now routinely refers juvenile cases to the Elders Council rather than sentencing them to county juvenile detention. The tribe has found that most juveniles prefer this resolution process. The juvenile must stipulate to the elements of the crime in order to participate.

The Integration of Native Traditions and Customs

Many native people and researchers contend that incarceration within a tribal setting allows the inmate to come to reconciliation with traditional values and thus limits recidivism. I asked the tribal detention administrators about the availability of traditional and cultural activities at Puyallup and Tohono O'odham facilities and the arrangements made by Lummi for its prisoners held in county detention.

The Puyallup custodial staff asserted that access to religious and ceremonial activities and sweat lodges was one of the reasons why the nation felt so strongly about the importance of having a tribal jail. The tribal police chief stated that the state of Washington handles incarceration very differently from the Puyallup Nation. The nation emphasizes diversion, treatment, and the continuation of family and community connections. Domestic violence and alcohol counseling programs are held at the jail. Ceremonies and sweats are held off-site at the tribal medical building, where inmates may participate if the tribal court agrees. When the tribal court wants a prisoner released for participation in a ceremony, the order is faxed to the jail and jail personnel provide transportation for the prisoner.

Reflections

Alternatives to incarceration are often perceived by tribal police as a more culturally compatible approach to punishment for crimes. Incarceration as a punishment was almost nonexistent prior to colonization. Western society is based on the concept of individual liberty, thus the deprivation of liberty is seen as the worst punishment that can be imposed. In traditional Indian societies, however, the focus is on the greatest good for the community. Restoration of harmony and restitution for the crime are the norm.

Indian communities that have followed the tradition of compensation and a restoration of harmony have emphasized alternatives to incarceration, thus keeping perpetrators within the community and stressing the need for them to accept responsibility for their actions. One study found that the number of persons in 1999 who were supervised in the community rather than being incarcerated rose by 8 percent over 1998.[35] Of those in alternative programs, 19 percent were electronically monitored, 14 percent were in home detention, 42 percent were sentenced to perform community service, 7 percent were required to report daily, and 15 percent were sentenced to other alternatives. The fact that almost half of those in alternative systems were required to perform community service underscores the attempt by tribal communities to emphasize restitution and a restoration of community harmony.

Alternatives to incarceration can provide a much less expensive means of holding wrongdoers accountable while preserving their place within the community. With functioning probation programs, and with substance abuse programs available in tribal communities, this approach can be easier for many tribal citizens to support than the idea of locking people up and throwing away the key.

11 Tribal Policing in Public Law 280 States

While law enforcement in Indian Country is generally a tribal or federal function, in some states it is conducted by state and tribal agencies pursuant to Public Law 280.[1] This federal statute, passed in 1953, has had an impact far beyond its actual text. Six states (Alaska, California, Minnesota, Nebraska, Oregon, and Wisconsin) were mandated to take jurisdiction over civil and criminal causes of action that occurred in Indian Country within their boundaries. Other states were allowed to assert jurisdiction if they chose to do so. This latter group, designated the "optional states," includes Washington and Montana, among others. A number of these optional states have taken an active approach to asserting state jurisdiction in Indian Country.

The states to be considered in this chapter are the six mandatory states (Alaska, California, Minnesota, Nebraska, Oregon, and Wisconsin) and the optional states (Florida, Montana, Nevada, Utah, and Washington). For a state-by-state overview of the status of PL 280, see table 11.1.

Tribal consent was not a requirement for the assertion of state authority for either the mandatory or optional states under the original legislation. Subsequent to the passage of this legislation, ten states accepted such jurisdiction. Then in 1968 Congress amended PL 280 to include a tribal consent requirement, which required a tribal referendum before states could assume jurisdiction. Since that date, no tribe has so consented.

Fundamental Principles of PL 280

In states that have assumed jurisdiction, PL 280 established state jurisdiction without abolishing tribal jurisdiction. Certain legal principles were established. These include the following:

- State and tribal powers are concurrent.
- The named states retain the same power to enforce their regular criminal laws inside Indian Country that they have always exercised outside of it.
- The states may not tax tribal governments for the services they provide.

Table 11.1   State-by-State Overview of the Status of Public Law 280

	Affected jurisdictions

Mandatory states

Alaska	All Indian Country within the state except the Annette Islands with regard to the Metlakatla Indians
California	All Indian Country within the state
Minnesota	All Indian Country within the state except Red Lake Reservation (retrocession accepted for Nett Lake Reservation)
Nebraska	All Indian Country within the state (retrocession accepted for Omaha Reservation)
Oregon	All Indian Country within the state except the Warm Springs Reservation (retrocession accepted for Umatilla Reservation)
Wisconsin	All Indian Country within the state (retrocession accepted for Menominee Reservation and Winnebago Indian Reservation)

Option states

Arizona	Air and water pollution
Florida	All Indian Country within the state
Idaho	Seven areas of subject matter jurisdiction. Full state jurisdiction if tribes consent: compulsory school attendance; juvenile delinquency and youth rehabilitation; dependent, neglected, and abused children; insanities and mental illness; public assistance; domestic relations; motor vehicle operation
Iowa	Civil jurisdiction over Sac and Fox Reservation
Montana	Criminal jurisdiction over Flathead Reservation. Full state jurisdiction where tribes request, counties consent, and governor proclaims (retrocession accepted for Salish and Kootenai Tribes)
Nevada	Full state jurisdiction, but counties may opt out; later amendment required tribal consent (retrocession accepted for all covered reservations)
North Dakota	Civil state jurisdiction only, subject to tribal consent
South Dakota	Criminal and civil matters arising on highways. Full state jurisdiction if United States reimburses costs of enforcement
Utah	Full state jurisdiction if tribes consent
Washington	Eight subject areas of jurisdiction on Indian trust land; full state jurisdiction as to non-Indians and Indians on nontrust land, although the state has allowed full retrocession fairly liberally (retrocession accepted for Confederated Tribes of the Chehalis Reservation, Quileute Reservation, Swinomish Tribal Community, Colville Indian Reservation, Port Madison and Quinault Reservation)

- The Federal Enclaves Act and the Major Crimes Act are wholly supplanted by the states.
- The states are not given regulatory powers over Indian Country, thus issues related to hunting and fishing rights on reservations can become very problematic. However, only regulations of general state applicability, not detailed local regulations, can be applied to the tribes.
- Gaming is regulatory. Thus, if gaming is permitted within the state, even though subject to regulation, the state must allow this activity in Indian Country. The regulations imposed by the state on permitted forms of gambling may not be applied to tribal gaming.

The Effect of Public Law 280

PL 280 is a vestige of the termination era of the 1950s, a time when the federal government was trying to "get out of the Indian Business." Using the excuse that there was rampant lawlessness in Indian Country, Congress gave the six mandated states extensive criminal and civil jurisdiction over Indian Country and permitted, for a time, all other states to acquire jurisdiction at their option. In those states where PL 280 was asserted, it fundamentally changed the balance of power in favor of the states.[2]

While PL 280 did not affect tribal criminal and civil jurisdiction, the widespread result was that tribal courts and law enforcement were seriously affected. PL 280, although separate from the termination/relocation process, came to be regarded as a termination of tribal jurisdiction. The retrocession process spelled out in the legislation, whereby states could give back their jurisdiction to the federal government, was largely overlooked.

Most tribes in PL 280 states allowed whatever tribal courts and law enforcement existed to wither and die. The federal status of many tribes was terminated in 1953 pursuant to House Concurrent Resolution 108. Federal funding for these tribes ceased. They thus were forced to look to state courts and county sheriffs to provide legal and law enforcement services. However, due to the fact that PL 280 did not allow the tribes to be taxed for the provision of such services, legal and law enforcement services were largely unavailable.

State law enforcement agencies generally ignored Indian Country, and even when requested by tribes, law enforcement was not provided.[3] Thus, as time passed, the problem of lawlessness in Indian Country within PL 280 states really did become extensive.[4] It generally took until the 1980s for tribes to act upon the fact that, while PL 280 had transferred federal jurisdiction to the designated states, it had not terminated tribal jurisdiction. It had simply made tribal and state jurisdiction concurrent.

It was then that tribal governments in PL 280 states began to look at ways to assert sovereignty and jurisdiction in order to take charge of the provision of law enforcement in Indian Country. Upon review it became evident that tribal civil and criminal jurisdiction could be asserted. The only necessary condition precedent to its implementation was the formation of tribal law enforcement departments and tribal courts. This became the mission of tribal governments wishing to assert sovereignty in this area.

Furthermore, since 1968, when Congress amended the act, states with PL 280 jurisdiction have been able to request retrocession of jurisdiction over individual tribes within their states. Pursuant to the approval of the secretary of the interior or through the passage of state legislation that requires tribal requests for jurisdiction be granted, PL 280 jurisdiction may be abandoned. While tribes may petition the state to request retrocession, the tribes have no official role in bringing the petition forward to the federal government. Should retrocession be granted, tribal jurisdiction over reservation Indians is determined according to general principles of federal Indian law.

The Assertion of Sovereignty

Sovereignty is an elusive concept. De jure sovereignty is asserted through the law, but to a great extent de facto sovereignty exists when it is believed in, treated as if it exists, and is vigorously asserted.

As tribal governments in PL 280 states faced increasing lawlessness, and states failed to provide adequate law enforcement services to tribal areas, tribes came to realize that if they were to contend with crime, they had to build law enforcement agencies for themselves. To do this they looked to federal sources for funding.

Federal funding, primarily from the Indian Self-Determination and Education Assistance Act of 1975 (Public Law 93-638), is now available to tribes in PL 280 states. Two sources of funding are available to tribes through this program. PL 93-638 is generally available only to tribes in PL 280 states that have achieved retrocession. However, in 1995, a tribal consortium in California was given a PL 93-638 contract to conduct a study on the feasibility of an intertribal court system.[5] A further problem with PL 93-638 funding is that it is on a contract basis with the Bureau of Indian Affairs. The receiving tribe is constrained in their use of this funding pursuant to the language of the particular contract.

The second source of federal funding from PL 93-638 has been more significant for tribes affected by PL 280. This funding flows from the self-governance program in this legislation. It is block grant funding and may be used by tribes for institutional purposes at their discretion.[6]

Third, many tribes in PL 280 states have used tribal funds to develop and maintain tribal law enforcement. As tribal economic development increases, this funding stream becomes highly significant. While self-governance compacts are relatively unrestricted and provide a high level of organizational freedom, the use of tribal funds allows tribes almost unconstrained tribal control of their law enforcement institutions.[7] These uses of federal and tribal funds have enabled tribes in PL 280 states to develop and implement tribal law enforcement services.

Findings from the Responding Tribes in Public Law 280 States

A total of ninety tribes responded to the national study in 2000. Of these, forty-nine were in PL 280 states. The forty-nine tribes varied widely. For example, while 6 of 7 tribes in Montana supplied data for the study, only 6 of 105 in California did so. To further this comparison, the Montana reservations are all geographically vast, with an average area of more than 1.25 million acres. The responding California tribes encompassed an average of 17,640 acres. This number is skewed, however, by the inclusion of the 85,000-acre Hoopa Reservation. If the Hoopa Reservation were excluded from the sample, the average area of the five remaining tribes that responded would be 689 acres.

The PL 280 tribes varied in size, population, and other characteristics. Their law enforcement departments' size, budget, and means of funding also vary. However, the tribes have some things in common. Funding of tribal law enforcement is predominantly on the shoulders of the individual tribes. It is relatively rare for tribes in PL 280 states to have any type of cooperative agreement with surrounding law enforcement agencies. This stands in dramatic contrast with the data obtained from all responding tribes (see table 11.2).

Funding for Tribal Law Enforcement

State funding of tribal law enforcement is rare. A total of fifteen of the forty-nine tribes indicated that they received state assistance through PL 280 for such services. The experiences of the tribes varied from California, where four of the six responding tribes reported receiving state police services through PL 280, to Nevada, where only one of seven tribes reported receiving state police services.

Table 11.2   Tribal Police Departments in Public Law 280 States

	Police departments	Employees	Cases (average)	Arrests (average)	Budget (average)
Alaska	1	1	—	—	—
California	6	45	3,367	167	$2,360,000
Florida	1	23	8,115	150	—
Minnesota	2	—	6,856	381	$1,500,000
Montana	5	25	5,052	1,619	$772,210
Nebraska	1	20	1,500	1,000	$650,000
Nevada	7	8	2,554	137	$439,220
Oregon	4	8	1,529	767	$581,666
Utah	1	18	2,000	200	$1,000,000
Washington	17	15	1,817	349	$607,975
Wisconsin	4	20	6,800	521	$1,132,645

The data from the ninety tribes indicated that a total of thirty-seven (41 percent) received PL 93-638 funding for tribal law enforcement services, twenty-three tribes (25 percent) allocated self-governance funding, eight (8 percent) received BIA funding, and twenty-five (28 percent) received Department of Justice COPS funding. Thirty-six tribes (40 percent) allocated tribal funding to tribal law enforcement; and thirteen (14 percent) tribal police departments were funded totally from tribal funds.

In comparison, data from the PL 280 tribes indicate that twenty-three tribes (47 percent) received PL 93-638 funding for tribal law enforcement services, thirty (61 percent) allocated self-governance funding, eleven (22 percent) received BIA funding, and eleven tribes (22 percent) received Department of Justice COPS funding. Thirty-two tribes (65 percent) allocated tribal funding to tribal law enforcement, thirteen (27 percent) were totally tribally funded, and 15 (31 percent) received state funding.

Thus the data indicate that most tribal law enforcement programs receive a mix of funding. However, tribes in PL 280 states allocate a disproportionate level of tribal funding to the provision of law enforcement services, either through the use of unrestricted self-governance funds or tribal funds. The possible ramification of this is that less funding may then be available for other tribal uses.

Tribal Codes and Ordinances

Of the ninety tribes, sixty-two responded regarding written criminal codes and protocols. Of these, fifty-eight indicated that their departments had written codes and protocols. All fifty-eight (94 percent) included ordinances related to the use of deadly force, forty-six (74 percent) included

Table 11.3   Written Tribal Codes and Protocols in Public Law 280 States

	Use of deadly force	Domestic violence	Misconduct complain procedures
Alaska	0	1	0
California	6	4	6
Florida	1	1	1
Minnesota	2	1	2
Montana	4	3	5
Nebraska	0	0	1
Nevada	6	7	4
Oregon	4	2	4
Utah	1	0	1
Washington	12	12	14
Wisconsin	3	3	4
Total	39	34	42

ordinances related to domestic violence, and fifty-three (85 percent) included formal protocols related to the handling of misconduct complaints.

Of the forty-nine PL 280 tribes that responded to the survey, forty-two
(86 percent) reported that their departments had written criminal codes
and ordinances. As shown in table 11.3, thirty-nine PL 280 tribes (80 percent) included ordinances related to the use of deadly force, thirty-four (69
percent) included ordinances related to domestic violence, and forty-two
(86 percent) included formal protocols related to the handling of misconduct
complaints.

Each sample has a large number of tribes that have written codes and
protocols. The national total of tribes having written codes related to both
use of deadly force and domestic violence is generally higher than when
only the PL 280 tribes are considered. Interestingly, however, both the
PL 280 tribes and the national sample have similar levels of formal protocols for the handling of citizen complaints.

Cooperation with Other Agencies

Unlike with mainstream policing, the issues of mutual-aid agreements
and cross-deputization are not settled in Indian Country, particularly in PL
280 states. When the PL 280 tribes are examined individually, however, the
numbers are markedly different. Of the forty-nine PL 280 tribes, twenty-
four (49 percent) had mutual-aid agreements, while fifty-seven (63 percent)
of the national sample had them. Of the PL 280 tribes, sixteen (33 percent)
had cross-deputized officers, while forty-three (48 percent) of the total national sample had them. An exception to this trend was Wisconsin, where

Table 11.4   Cooperation with Surrounding Agencies

	Responding Tribes	Cross-deputization				Mutual aid			
		Tribal	City police	County sheriff	State police	Tribal	City police	County sheriff	State police
Alaska	1	0	1	0	0	0	0	0	0
California	6	0	0	1	0	1	1	1	1
Florida	1	0	0	1	0	0	1	1	1
Minnesota	2	0	0	0	0	0	0	1	0
Montana	5	0	0	0	0	0	1	1	1
Nebraska	1	0	0	0	1	0	0	0	—
Nevada	7	0	1	0	0	2	2	3	1
Oregon	4	0	0	3	0	0	1	2	2
Utah	1	0	0	0	0	0	0	1	0
Washington	17	2	3	8	0	3	6	6	2
Wisconsin	—	0	0	2	0	1	2	4	0

the responding tribes all indicated that they had mutual-aid agreements with the county sheriff, and Washington state, where half of the responding tribes indicated that they had cross-deputization agreements with the county sheriff (see table 11.4).

Mutual-Aid Agreements

When the PL 280 tribes are examined separately from the national sample, the percentages of tribes with mutual-aid agreements are significantly lower across the board. Here the data indicate that seven (14 percent) had existing mutual-aid agreements with other tribal police departments, fourteen (29 percent) with city police, twenty (41 percent) with county sheriff's departments, and eight (16 percent) with state police. The national sample reflected that of the total, nineteen tribes (21 percent) had existing mutual-aid agreements with other tribal police departments, thirty (33 percent) with city police, fifty-two (58 percent) with county sheriff's departments, and nineteen (21 percent) with state police.

The numbers for mutual-aid agreements between tribal police departments, between city police departments and tribes, and between state police and tribal police are not markedly different overall. However, the number of agreements with county sheriff's departments in PL 280 states, when compared with the overall total, is very different. Here far more tribes in the national sample had mutual-aid agreements with county sheriffs than did tribes in PL 280 states. This is a very disturbing statistic, particularly given the relationship that should exist between tribes and county sheriffs when the state has criminal and civil jurisdiction in Indian Country. The infrequency of mutual-aid agreements gives support to the lack of trust expressed by tribal officers, discussed later in this chapter.

Cross-Deputization

The data related to cross-deputization of tribal law enforcement nationwide and in PL 280 states indicate that it is even less frequent than mutual aid. It is rare for individual tribal law enforcement officers to be cross-deputized, and it is even rarer for officers in PL 280 states. While cross-deputization was much more frequent with city, county, and state law enforcement in the national sample, it was less frequent in regard to tribal police departments. More than twice as many tribes in the nationwide survey had officers cross-deputized with other tribal police departments than did PL 280 tribes.

The data from the national survey indicate that approximately eight tribes (9 percent) employed officers who were cross-deputized with other tribal police departments, seven (8 percent) with city police, thirty-one (34 percent) with county sheriffs, and nine (10 percent) with state police.

The PL 280 states sample indicates that only two tribes (4 percent) reported that their officers were cross-deputized with other tribal police departments, five (10 percent) with city police, fifteen (31 percent) with county sheriffs, and only one (2 percent) with state police.

With cross-deputization, the most significant difference was with state police. While both numbers were extremely low, 10 percent of tribes in the national survey employed officers who were cross-deputized with state police, while only 2 percent of the PL 280 employed such officers. This again raises the issue of cooperation (or lack thereof) between tribal and state agencies in PL 280 states, a particularly egregious situation where states have law enforcement responsibilities in Indian Country.

Issues for Cross-Deputization and Mutual-Aid Agreements

The tribes were queried about any problems that existed with other agencies regarding cross-deputization and mutual aid. Sixteen tribes responded to this question, five of these in PL 280 states. All five of the PL 280 tribes and most of the national sample cited problems with the county sheriff that centered on a lack of trust. A number stated that their agreements were unwritten and that they had difficulty holding the county sheriffs to the agreement. In general, the relationships between tribal law enforcement in PL 280 states and surrounding county agencies were not easy.

Reflections

The data obtained and discussed in this chapter are influenced by the fact that approximately 50 percent of the tribes that responded to the 2000 survey were located in PL 280 states. Further, the large majority of the responses were from only a few PL 280 states. For example, while there were only six respondents from among California's ninety-five separate reservations, seventeen of the twenty-six tribes in Washington completed the survey. Seven of twenty-six Nevada tribes responded, as did five of the seven Montana tribes. Four of the ten Oregon tribes responded, as did four of the eleven Wisconsin tribes.

It is an interesting question as to why so many tribes from the relatively few PL 280 states responded. Perhaps one reason was that these tribes were simply happy to be considered. Relationships between states and tribes can be difficult, and relatively few opportunities exist for input and feedback on issues facing tribes.

The problem facing tribes in PL 280 states is dramatic. The states generally fail to provide adequate law enforcement services to tribes within their boundaries due to a number of factors, including the inability of the states to tax Indian tribes, the budgetary and staffing constraints facing the states generally, and the pervasive problems inherent in the relationship between local jurisdictions and tribal governments.

PL 280 tribes that wish to address the provision of law enforcement themselves may do so, as their jurisdiction is concurrent with the state. However, they must generally provide their own funding either through tribal funds or self-government funding.

The sample further indicates that the PL 280 tribes are less likely to have written codes and ordinances and are less likely to have mutual-aid or cross-deputization agreements with surrounding law enforcement agencies or with the state police.

The challenges faced by tribes that make the decision to assert sovereignty and provide law enforcement services to their citizens are large but not insurmountable. It is incumbent for PL 280 tribes to increase their application for federal funding to assist them in this endeavor. PL 93-638 contracts should be sought, and they should apply for other federal law enforcement grants. The earmarking of tribal funds should continue, as these funds are unconstrained. Furthermore, the tribes should do their utmost to develop and implement mutual-aid and cross-deputization agreements with surrounding law enforcement agencies. The issue of tribal sovereignty is important, but so is the increase in safety and support for tribal officers that could result. Tribes must do everything possible to resolve their differences with surrounding law enforcement agencies in order to implement agreements that are both culturally and professionally acceptable.

Tribal policing is an important factor in the safety of reservation residents. The departments must be empowered to do their jobs. Unfortunately, as the situation now exists, tribes in PL 280 states are faced with the choice of having essentially no law enforcement or providing their own. PL 280 tribes should vigorously pursue retrocession with the state. As evidenced by the statistics related to mutual aid and cross-deputization, and the comments made by surveyed officers and tribal police departments, the relationships between tribes and PL 280 states are not particularly good. This point alone should encourage tribes to pursue retrocession. This pursuit can take many forms, from tribal legal action to require adequate police protection by state officers to political lobbying and advocacy with state officials and appeals to public conscience. The decision about what form the approach should take is best left up to the individual tribe. Many states now have declining budgets and difficulty providing adequate police services to their other citizens, let alone those in Indian Country. While achieving retrocession may be difficult, it is essential that tribes use this window of opportunity to engage in the struggle to assert jurisdiction and to enhance tribal sovereignty. Retrocession of PL 280 jurisdiction must be pursued.

12 Conclusion

What does it mean to be a tribal police officer? What are the intricacies of this role? How do the tribal communities, tribal police departments, and other law enforcement agencies interact to effectively address the serious issues of violence, crime, and criminality in Indian Country? The answers to these questions are as varied as are American Indian tribal communities. Some essential elements, however, lie at the core of a new paradigm for law enforcement in Indian Country: service, sovereignty, tradition, and competency.

Tribal policing arises out of a tradition of service to Indian communities. From precolonial times, those chosen accepted responsibility for the safety, protection, and order of the community. They lived and worked as a part of their communities and were held accountable by those communities. Though there may have been changes in the form of tribal policing after colonization, the personal sense of responsibility and the community expectation of responsibility and accountability did not alter.

Over the centuries of contact with European immigrants and their descendants, the form of tribal policing changed. From the traditional clan, warrior, and policing societies came the traditional members of Indian communities who served in reservation and federal police agencies. The traditional leadership of Indian communities continued its commitment to service and to the safety of the people even when that service was under the direction of federal authorities. Traditional leaders of clan, warrior, and policing societies lent their authority, their prestige, and their political influence to the creation of tribal police, thus easing their communities' transition onto reservations.

Now this tradition of leadership and authority has passed to a new generation of tribal police who work for the tribes themselves and who continue to ensure the safety of Indian people. While the form may have changed, the commitment has not. Tribal police officers continue to carry this tradition forward.

The commitment of tribal police and their interest in helping others to understand the intricacies of law enforcement was evident throughout the research for this book. Tribal officers serve Indian communities even though they may face difficult challenges. High crime rates, inadequate administrative infrastructure, low pay, difficult terrain, and a lack of material resources such as working police cars, radios, phone service, and lack of promotional opportunities all serve to hinder officers.

Despite these disadvantages, trained officers remain in tribal policing because it is the fulfillment of the idea of the "useful person." In most tribes, to be considered a useful person is the ultimate compliment. Being of service when asked and volunteering for difficult tasks are the traditional measures of a person. It is these ideas that motivate tribal officers and inspire tribal citizens to make tribal law enforcement their goal.

Additionally, there is the desire of Indian people and governments to be truly sovereign and self-governing. This desire permeates Indian Country even though there may be legal and administrative obstacles. Most tribal administrators and tribal citizens view a well-functioning tribal police agency as an essential aspect of self-government. Tribal police serve as the juncture of sovereignty and justice on a daily basis.

The obstacles that arise from the assertion of sovereignty and self-government can be significant. While the era in which we live is ostensibly one of self-determination, the tribes face many legal, administrative, and financial challenges. These challenges must be considered and overcome if tribal policing is to be fully successful.

Many of the legal challenges to Indian policing are a vestige of an age when the federal government believed that Indian justice was primitive and incomprehensible. For example, U.S. Supreme Court Justice William Rehnquist cited the 1883 *Ex Parte Crow Dog* case in 1975 when considering tribal criminal jurisdiction over non-Indian residents of a reservation. Justice Rehnquist and a majority of the Court held that such jurisdiction was legally impermissible even though adequate mainstream police services are generally unavailable to Indian Country. Tribal police and judges struggle against this tradition of colonizing thought every day. This struggle is crucial if Indian Country is to successfully deal with the crime rate on reservations.

Some tribes have begun to define tribal criminal jurisdiction broadly and to assert jurisdiction over non-Indian wrongdoers in lieu of actions by federal law enforcement agencies. Other tribes aggressively assert civil jurisdiction over non-Indian wrongdoers through the use of civil penalties, including fines and banishment from tribal lands. Some tribes assert felony jurisdiction over Indian wrongdoers where otherwise federal jurisdiction through the Major Crimes Act (or state jurisdiction in PL 280 states) would prevail. In these situations — including, for example, the Navajo and Salt

River Pima tribes—tribal criminal justice systems, rather than charging wrongdoers with felonies, assert jurisdiction through the charging of separate lesser-included misdemeanors, resulting in the stacking of charges, expanded criminal jurisdiction, and more extensive criminal penalties.

Tribes often find that educated, experienced personnel are scarce and difficult to recruit. The attrition rate for trained personnel is very high, with people often leaving for more highly paid positions in the non-Indian community. Codes, ordinances, and administrative procedures are costly to develop and implement, leaving many tribes with inadequate rule structures. How can these administrative and personnel challenges be addressed? One logical answer is for the tribe to develop and educate tribal citizens itself.

Many tribes have high schools and tribal colleges on tribal lands. Tribal citizens find that these institutions make education more accessible and are conducive to improving their skills. Some tribal law enforcement agencies—for example, that of the Pascua Yaqui in Arizona—have begun to develop police cadet programs for high school students. These programs allow young people to develop the skills, background, and outlook necessary to move successfully into careers in law enforcement. They re-create for the young the roles of community guardian and law keeper that were so much a part of traditional Indian societies. They also reestablish the role of elders in the education and guidance of the young. Many tribes have found that women move more easily than young men into law enforcement roles, perhaps as a logical extension of their role as caregivers. These police cadet programs can give young people, particularly young men, a role founded traditionally in a guardian and warrior tradition, a role of which they can be proud.

Tribal colleges have begun to develop associate of arts and bachelor of arts degrees in the fields of the administration of justice and criminal justice. These colleges, with an emphasis on enlightened justice studies, can serve as the foundation for the new paradigm of tribal policing. Further, public administration courses taught at the tribal college level could be highly useful in producing skilled administrative officials whose focus could be on the development of innovative codes and protocols. Internships should be developed in tribal governments to assist Indian people and interested non-Indians in learning about tribal governments while doing a significant service for Indian Country.

Financially, these are difficult times in Indian Country. Many tribal citizens live below the poverty line, and the costs of tribal infrastructure are high. Federal monies for programs are scarce, and tribes have to compete with states and municipalities for funding. Often there are competing priorities. In PL 280 states, tribes have been subject to state jurisdiction and have been led to believe that tribal justice jurisdiction no longer exists.

But there are new opportunities. Many tribes have gaming facilities, and a few are very successful. Tribes with successful gaming facilities often use the resulting funds to support the administrative services and infrastructure of the tribe. Tribal law enforcement is commonly the recipient of such funding.

Many tribes also have undertaken tribally and privately funded economic development programs that have become financially successful. These economic endeavors may employ many tribal members, thus raising the standard of living on reservations. Often funding from these programs is also used to develop accountable justice systems, which then enhance economic development as outside investors gain confidence that any disputes they may have with the tribe will be fairly and impartially addressed. Tribes in PL 280 states have developed law enforcement and tribal courts that exercise jurisdiction concurrently with state agencies.

As the tribes create new tribal police departments and enhance those that already exist, opportunities abound. Lessons learned from mainstream policing (e.g., the value of diversity, the development of community policing and accountability, and the use of appropriate technology) can enhance the development of tribal police. Tribal traditions of law enforcement and protection of the community can serve as touchstones for modern tribal police. The traditions and experiences of policing in the various tribal communities can inform other developing programs. The community policing approach is a natural fit in Indian Country and can serve as a model for mainstream police departments that want to join with their communities in problem solving. In all, prototypes can develop and grow. New ways of coping with difficult situations can arise. All can learn from one another.

An essential part of this growth is the inclusion of a variety of voices in tribal policing. Beyond the role of women in policing, there is the frequent inclusion of community members in safety committees and accountability systems. There is also an established role for experts with experience in mainstream and tribal justice. Because these other parties reflect both the tribal and the mainstream communities and because tribal communities tend to favor grassroots activism on issues of tribal concern, tribal police and policies reflect the best of both worlds.

The enhancement of tribal sovereignty through the provision of law enforcement services depends on tribal governments moving from BIA police to tribal police. Through the use of PL 93-638 contracts and HR 4872 self-governance funding, as well as tribal funds, truly responsive and accountable tribal police departments can develop and flourish.

Both non-Indian policing and tribal policing have important roles in Indian Country. They help and support each other. They learn from each other. They serve as essential components of the safety of tribal members. Together they serve both tribal communities and those communities that border on Indian Country.

Tribal police departments created by the tribal community, coupled with community concerns and input, the cutting-edge approach of knowledgeable experts, and support from federal and state agencies will create the new paradigm of tribal policing — a paradigm that sees law enforcement not just as crime fighters but as an arm of restorative justice and the rehabilitation of wrongdoers. Tribal policing, the heart of the tribal legal system, is the juncture of tribal sovereignty and justice.

NOTES

Introduction

1. For more on the discussion of de jure and de facto sovereignty, see Cornell and Kalt 1992. There, the authors set forth the fundamental premise that tribes have the right to make decisions that assert self-determination for themselves, rather than awaiting a court's determination of their right to undertake certain actions. These concepts of de facto and de jure sovereignty, as defined and advanced by Cornell and Kalt, will be used throughout this book.

2. For more on this see Luna 1997, 1998.

Chapter 1. Policing in Indian Country

1. See *Colliflower v. Garland*, 342 F. 2d 369 (1965).

2. *Talton v. Mayes*, 163 U.S. 376 (1896).

3. *Cherokee Nation v. Georgia*, 30 U.S. [5 Pet.] 1 and *Worcester v. Georgia*, 31 U.S. [6 Pet.] 515.

4. *U.S. v. Kagama*, 118 U.S. 375 (1886).

5. *Worcester v. Georgia*, 31 U.S. [6 Pet.] 515.

6. Canby 2004, 109–17.

7. See, for example, *Arizona v. California*, 373 U.S. 546 (1963).

8. U.S. 375 (1886).

9. USCA 1153.

10. U.S. 553 (1903).

11. U.S. 556.

12. Public Law 93-638, 88 Stat. 2203.

13. H.R. 4842.

14. This and the following information regarding the number of law enforcement agencies of different types operating in Indian Country was obtained from the U.S. Bureau of Indian Affairs (1995).

15. Reno 1995.

16. Kress 1996.

17. The Major Crimes Act (18 USCA 1153) grants jurisdiction to the federal government over the following crimes: murder, manslaughter, assault with intent to commit murder, kidnapping, rape, statutory rape, assault with intent to commit rape, incest, assault with a dangerous weapon, assault resulting in serious bodily injury, arson, burglary, robbery, and larceny.

18. Luna 1998.

19. "Ariz. Reservations See More Killings" (2003).

20. *Oliphant v. Suquamish Indian Tribe*, 435 U.S. 191.

21. Wakeling et al. 2000, 42.

2. The History of the Tribal Police

1. Hagan 1980, 25.
2. Strickland 1975, 68.
3. Ibid., 104.
4. Ibid., 185–86.
5. Ellis 1999, 186–87.
6. Ibid., 189.
7. Ibid., 199–200.
8. Ibid., 195.
9. Tate 1977, 101.
10. Ibid., 26.
11. See, for example, Circular Letter of June 10, 1869, from H. L. Crosby of the U.S. Department of the Interior, National Archives, Washington, DC.
12. Barlow 1994, 146.
13. Jones 1966, 230.
14. Ibid., 235–36.
15. Ibid.; Tate 1977, 106.
16. Tate 1977, 111.
17. Ibid.; Barlow 1994, 141, quoting David Roberts, "Geronimo," *National Geographic* 182 (October 1992): 58.
18. Barlow 1994, 147.
19. See, for example, S. A. Blain, U.S. Agent, to General Sam Houston, June 10, 1860, and Special Order No. 34, from the Secretary of War to Lt. Col. A. Clendennin, archives of the Center for American History, University of Texas, Austin.
20. See, for example, Moses Wiley, Wheeler County Attorney, to John B. Jones, Adj. Gen. of Texas August 14, 1879, archives of the Center for American History, University of Texas, Austin.
21. Hagan 1980, 42.
22. Ibid., 43.
23. Hagan 1980, 48.
24. U.S. Bureau of Indian Affairs 1975, 24.
25. Ibid., 69.
26. Ibid.; Hagan 1980, 51.
27. U.S. Bureau of Indian Affairs 1975, 10, 69.
28. See, for example, Commissioner of Department of the Interior, Office of Indian Affairs, to Captain Frank K. Baldwin, Acting Indian Agent, Kiowa Agency, December 26, 1894, archives of the Center for American History, University of Texas, Austin. The letter denies a request to spend $150 to purchase corn for the subsistence of police horses and the right to hire horses for police use when necessary.
29. See, for example, Commissioner of the Department of the Interior, Office of Indian Affairs, to Charles K. Adams, U.S. Indian Agent, Kiowa Agency, March 28, 1891, archives of the Center for American History, University of Texas, Austin. The letter denies the purchase of leg irons and Winchesters for use in the Indian service. See also Commissioner of the Department of the Interior, Office of Indian Affairs, to Capt. H. G. Brown, Acting Indian Agent for the Kiowa Agency, September 15, 1893.
30. Ibid.; Hagan 1980, 80–81.

31. Stat. 388 et sec.

32. Stat. 497 et sec.

33. Ibid.; U.S. Bureau of Indian Affairs 1975, 14.

34. U.S. Bureau of Indian Affairs 1975, 45.

35. Ibid., 56.

36. Ibid., 70–71.

Chapter 3. Legal Institutions and Structures

1. For an in-depth discussion of this topic, see Canby 1998, 62–71.

2. Fed 575 (1888).

3. U.S. 557 (1883).

4. Stat. 385 (1885).

5. U.S. 375 (1886).

6. U.S. 641 (1977).

7. U.S. 621 (1881).

8. U.S. 191 (1978).

9. U.S. 313 (1978).

10. U.S. 676 (1990).

11. USCA sec. 1301(2).

12. U.S. 193.

13. U.S. 353 (2001).

Chapter 4. Indian Country Jurisdictional Issues

1. Clinton 1976.

2. Canby 1998, 125.

3. USCA sec. 1153.

4. USCA sec. 1153.

5. USCA sec. 1152.

6. *Solem v. Bartlett*, 465 U.S. 463, 465n2.

7. U.S. 193 (2004).

8. *Indian L. Rep.* 6083 (Navajo S. Ct. 1999).

9. *Settler v. Lameer*, 507 F. 2d 231 (9th Cir. 1974); see also *New Mexico v. Mescalero Apache Tribe*, 462 U.S. 324 (1983).

10. *Montana v. U.S. Environmental Protection Agency*, 137 F. 3d 1135 (9th Cir. 1998); see also *City of Albuquerque v. Browner*, 97 F. 3d 415 (10th Cir. 1996).

11. *Brendale v. Confederated Tribes and Bands of the Yakima Indian Nation*, 492 U.S. 408 (1989).

12. *Montana v. U.S.*, 450 U.S. 544 (1981).

13. USC 1161.

14. Indian Gaming Regulatory Act of 1988, 25 USCA secs. 2701–21, 18 USCA sec. 1166.

15. *Ex Parte Crow Dog*, 109 U.S. 556 (1883) and the Major Crimes Act, 18 USCA sec. 1153.

16. The relatively rare incidence of cross-deputization relates to the fact that most states and municipalities require an officer to be state certified in order to be cross-

deputized. This presents a difficulty in Indian Country, where relatively few officers are state certified. Often the only tribal officers who meet this standard have been hired from state or municipal jurisdictions and have brought their state certification with them.

17. F. 2d 683, 9th Cir. 1969.

18. U.S. 353 (2001).

19. *Montana v. U.S.*, 450 U.S. 544 (1981).

Chapter 5. Tribal Policing Models

1. Portions of this chapter were previously published in a chapter in Jeffrey Ian Ross and Larry Gould, eds., *Native Americans and the Criminal Justice System: Theoretical and Policy Directions,* 117–34, © 2006 by Paradigm Publishers.

2. Walker 1998a.

3. Walker 1999.

4. Walker 1977.

5. Ibid.

6. Luna 1999.

7. Canby 2004, 182–85.

8. U.S. 375, 6 S. Ct. 1109, 30 L. Ed. 228 (1886).

9. U.S. 553, 23 S. Ct. 216, 47 L. Ed. 299 (1903).

10. Luna 1997.

11. Research conducted by Luna and Walker (1997). Information obtained from this study serves as the basis for the data to be found throughout this chapter.

12. U.S. 44 (1996).

13. S. 2298, American Indian Civil Rights Enforcement Act; S. 2299, American Indian Contract Enforcement Act; S. 2300, State Excise Sales and Transactions Enforcement Act of 1998; S. 2301, Tribal Environmental Accountability Act; and S. 2302, American Indian Tort Liability Insurance Act, all require the waiver of tribal sovereign immunity as necessary to enforce the acts.

14. For more on this topic, see Wakeling 2000, 16–19.

15. Ibid., 17. The data in this table are derived from the U.S. Bureau of Indian Affairs 1995.

16. USC sec. 1162.

17. The effect of HCR 108 was to terminate the federal status of many tribes and place their land under state, rather than federal, jurisdiction. The effect of this legislation is seen today throughout California, for example, where many tribes and rancherias have yet to regain federal recognition.

18. For more on the subject of Public Law 280 see Goldberg-Ambrose 1997.

19. See DiGregory and Manuel 1997 for the comment on a "chronic shortage of personnel" in Indian Country law enforcement agencies.

20. DiGregory and Manuel 1997.

21. Wakeling et al. 2000, 42.

22. Ibid., 36–37.

23. DiGregory and Manuel 1997.

24. Wakeling et al. 2000, 26.

25. The 1980 U.S. Census figures revealed that the percentage of reservation-

based American Indians over the age of sixteen who were employed was slightly higher (65 percent) than the percentage of the general population (62 percent), although the income levels were significantly lower. The median family income in 1980 for reservation-based American Indians was $9,920, and 45 percent were living below the poverty threshold of $7,412. This compares negatively to the general population median income of $19,920, and to only 12 percent of the general population who were living below the poverty threshold in 1980.

26. The 1980 U.S. Census figures revealed that only 43 percent of American Indians over the age of twenty-five who resided on reservations were high school graduates, as compared with 67 percent of all Americans.

27. *Morton v. Mancari*, 417 U.S. 535 (1974).

28. Cornell and Kalt 1992.

29. The federal COPS program contends that there are five essential elements necessary for law enforcement to become culturally competent: (1) value diversity, (2) have the capacity for cultural self-assessment, (3) be conscious of dynamics inherent when cultures interact, (4) gain cultural knowledge, and (5) adapt to diversity. These elements are provided to law enforcement agencies as part of the COPS Information kit.

30. Community Policing Consortium 1997, chap. 3.

31. Ibid.

Chapter 6. Training Tribal Law Enforcement Personnel

1. For more on this topic, see Luna-Firebaugh 2005.

2. Maniaci 2005.

Chapter 7. Infrastructure Challenges

1. Johnson 2000.

2. Rolo 2000.

3. Ibid.

4. Johnson 2000.

5. Feinman 1986, 198.

6. Shirley 2005b.

7. Shirley 2005a.

8. For example, the Comprehensive Indian Resources for Community and Law Enforcement (CIRCLE) Project funded by the National Institute of Justice, 2002–4. Research conducted by the Udall Center and Harvard University. This author focused on the Northern Cheyenne.

9. Rolo 2000.

Chapter 8. Women in Tribal Policing

1. An earlier form of this chapter was published in the *Social Science Journal* 39 (2002): 583–92; reprinted with permission from Elsevier.

2. Walker, Spohn, and DeLone 1996.

3. Martin 1994.

4. Turner 1996.
5. Martin 1994.
6. Maniaci 2005.
7. Ibid.
8. Fletcher 1995.
9. Martin 1992.

Chapter 9. Police Accountability in the Indian Community

1. An earlier form of this chapter was published in the *Georgetown Public Policy Review* 4 (Spring 1999): 149–64.

2. Civilian review boards were in existence in some major cities during the 1960s. The oldest continuously functioning civilian review board in the United States is the Police Review Commission (PRC) of Berkeley, California. The PRC was established by a voter initiative in 1972.

3. Walker 1998c.

4. See, for example, Luna and Walker 1997.

5. Information obtained by research conducted by the author. Although the terms "civilian review" and "citizen review" are generally used in the non-Indian community, the terms "community review" or "community oversight" seem more appropriate for Indian Country and thus will be used in reference to oversight systems for American Indian tribal police.

6. Barker 1998.

7. Ibid., viii.

8. Harring 1982, 102.

9. Clem and Rumbolz 1982, 68.

10. Brunet 1993, Sowers 1998, Wagner 1997, Walsh 1998.

11. Greenfeld and Smith 1999.

12. For more on sovereignty in general see Getches, Wilkinson, and Williams 2005 and Cohen 1982. For more on sovereignty as it relates to American Indian tribal police, see Luna 1998.

13. Portions of this section were first published in Luna 1998.

14. Some of the tribal police departments in PL 280 states that were queried for this study include Fort Hall in Idaho and Lac du Flambeau in Wisconsin (Goldberg-Ambrose 1995).

15. Amnesty International 1998, 47.

16. Walker and Wright 1995.

17. Walker 1998b.

18. Including those done by academics such as Samuel Walker 1998c, Andrew Goldsmith 1991 and Douglas Perez 1994, and studies funded and published by the cities of Albuquerque, NM (1997), Tucson, AZ (1996), and Portland, OR (1993), among others.

19. Luna 1998.

20. Muckleshoot and Rosebud.

21. Pine Ridge, Lac Du Flambeau, Spirit Lake, Menominee, White River, Fort Hall, Kickapoo, Cheyenne-Arapaho, Muckleshoot, Saint Regis Mohawk, Muskogee Creek, Rosebud, Lummi, and Fort Peck.

22. Mohegan and Omaha.

23. Pueblo of Santa Ana, Rocky Boy's, San Carlos, Navajo, Hannahville, and Cheyenne River.

24. Fort Peck.

25. See, for example, Luna and Walker 1997, Walker and Wright Kreisel 1996, and ACLU 1992.

26. Information obtained through research conducted by the author.

27. Muckleshoot tribe in Washington.

28. Kickapoo and White River.

29. Menominee and Lummi.

30. Fort Hall.

31. Cheyenne Arapaho, Hannahville, and Fort Peck.

32. Saint Regis Mohawk.

33. Examples abound of this troubled relationship between police and civilian oversight systems, from frequent lawsuits filed by police associations to individual refusals by police officers to cooperate. For more on this subject see ACLU 1992. Quotation from Walker 1992, 290.

34. Barker 1998, 93.

35. Amnesty International 1998, 47–49.

36. Ibid., 48.

37. Luna and Walker 1997, 122–124.

Chapter 10. Tribal Jails and Corrections

1. An earlier form of this chapter was published in *Prison Journal* 83 (March 2003): 1–16.

2. U.S. Department of the Interior, Office of Inspector General 2004, 10.

3. The 2000 report is entitled "Jails in Indian Country, 1998 and 1999." Greenfield and Smith 1999, Ditton 2000.

4. Ibid.

5. Greenfeld and Smith 1999.

6. Ibid.; Ditton 2000.

7. USCA sec. 1153.

8. Stat. 588.

9. Ditton 2000.

10. U.S. Department of the Interior, Office of Inspector General 2004, 50–51.

11. Ibid., 26.

12. Ibid., 32.

13. Ibid., chap. 5.

14. Ibid., 52.

15. *Santa Clara Pueblo v. Martinez*, 436 U.S. 49, 58 (1978).

16. Stat. 77, 25 USCA sec. 1301 et seq.

17. *United States v. Lester*, 647 F. 2d, 869 (8th Cir. 1981).

18. *Rhodes v. Chapman*, 452 U.S. 337, 346 (1981).

19. *Ramos v. Lamm*, 639 F. 2d 559, 566 (10th Circ. 1980), cert. Den., 450 U.S. 1041 (Apr. 1981).

20. *Ramos*, at 566.

21. *Estelle v. Gamble*, 429 U.S. 97, 102 (1976).

22. *Ruiz v. Estelle*, 666 F. 2d 854 (5th Cir.), cert. Den., 460 U.S. 1042 (1982).

23. PL 93-638, 88 Stat. 2203.

24. Code of Federal Regulations sec. 11.305 (1991).

25. Ditton 2000.

26. Ibid.

27. Coalition for Juvenile Justice 2000, 14.

28. Ibid.

29. Ibid.

30. Ibid.

31. Ibid.

32. Martin and Alese 1995.

33. U.S. Department of the Interior, Office of Inspector General 2004, 45–47.

34. Ibid., 55.

35. Ditton 2000.

Chapter 11. Tribal Policing in Public Law 280 States

1. USC Sec. 1162.

2. Canby 1998, 216.

3. This author was involved as an attorney for tribes in several incidents in California where county law enforcement services were requested by tribes and refused (e.g., enforcement of a restraining order, eviction of a squatter on Indian lands, etc.).

4. Goldberg-Ambrose 1997, 10–12.

5. Ibid., 200.

6. Ibid.

7. Wakeling et al. 2001, 8; *Ex Parte Crow Dog*, 109 U.S. 556; *Oliphant v. Suquamish Indian Tribe*, 435 U.S. 191.

REFERENCES

Archival Sources

Center for American History, University of Texas, Austin. U.S. Department of the Interior, Office of Indian Affairs, Correspondence, 1860–1894.

National Archives and Records Administration, Southwest Region, Dallas–Fort Worth, Texas. U.S. Department of the Interior, Bureau of Indian Affairs, Records, 1975.

National Archives and Records Administration, Washington, D.C. U.S. Department of the Interior, Office of Indian Affairs, Correspondence, 1869.

Published Sources

American Civil Liberties Union (ACLU). 1992. *Fighting Police Abuse: A Community Action Manual.* New York: ACLU Department of Public Education.

Amnesty International. 1998. *United States of America: Rights for All.* London: Amnesty International Publications.

"Ariz. Reservations See More Killings." 2003. *Arizona Daily Star*, October 8.

Barker, Michael L. 1998. *Policing in Indian Country.* New York: Harrow and Heston.

Barker, M., and K. Mullen. 1993. "Cross-Deputization in Indian Country." *Police Studies* 16 (4): 14–32.

Barlow, David E. 1994. "Minorities Policing Minorities as a Strategy of Social Control: A Historical Analysis of Tribal Police in the United States." *Criminal Justice History* 15: 142.

Brunet, Robin. 1993. "Intimidated by Indians." *Alberta Report* 20 (3): 19.

Canby, William C. 1998. *American Indian Law.* St. Paul, MN: West Group.

———. 2004. *American Indian Law in a Nutshell.* 4th ed. St. Paul, MN: West Publishing Co.

City of Tucson. 1996. *External Police Review: A Discussion of Existing City of Tucson Procedures and Alternative Models.* October 7. Tucson, AZ: City of Tucson.

Clem, Alan L., and James Rumbolz. 1982. *Law Enforcement: The South Dakota Experience.* Sturgis, SD: South Dakota Peace Officers Association.

Clinton, Robert N. 1976. "Criminal Jurisdiction over Indian Lands: A Journey through a Jurisdictional Maze." *Arizona Law Review* 18:503.

Coalition for Juvenile Justice. 2000. *Enlarging the Healing Circle: Ensuring Justice for American Indian Children.* Report on Racial Inequality. Washington, DC.

Cohen, F. S. 1982. *Handbook of Federal Indian Law.* Albuquerque: University of New Mexico Press.

Community Policing Consortium. 1997. "To Protect and Serve: An Overview of Community Policing on Indian Reservations," MS, U.S. Department of Justice, Office of Community Policing Services, Washington, DC.

Cornell, Stephen, and Joseph P. Kalt. 1992. "Reloading the Dice." In *What Can Tribes Do?* ed. Stephen Cornell and Joseph P. Kalt, 1–59. Los Angeles: University of California, American Indian Studies Center.

DiGregory, Kevin, and Hilda Manuel. 1997. *Report of the Executive Committee for Indian Country Law Enforcement Improvements to the U.S. Attorney General and the Secretary of the Interior.* U.S. Department of Justice, Criminal Division, Washington, DC.

Ditton, P. M. 2000. *Jails in Indian Country, 1998 and 1999.* NCJ 173410. Washington, DC: U.S. Department of Justice, Office of Justice Programs, Bureau of Justice Statistics. July.

Ellis, Mark. R. 1999. "Reservation Akicitas: The Pine Ridge Indian Police, 1879–1885." *South Dakota History* 29 (Fall): 185–210.

Etheridge, David. 1977. "Law Enforcement on Indian Reservations." *Police Chief* (April): 74–77.

Feinman, Clarice. 1986. "Police Problems on the Navajo Reservation." *Police Studies* 9 (Winter): 194–98.

Fletcher, C. 1995. *Breaking and Entering: Women Cops Talk about Life in the Ultimate Men's Club.* New York: HarperCollins.

Frederick, Calvin J. 1973. *Suicide, Homicide, and Alcoholism among American Indians.* National Institute of Mental Health, Division of Special Mental Health Programs, Center for Studies of Crime and Delinquency. Washington, DC: U.S. Government Printing Office.

Friedman, Lawrence M. 1985. *A History of American Indian Law.* 2d ed. New York: Simon and Schuster.

Getches, D., C. Wilkinson, and R. Williams. 1993. *Federal Indian Law.* 4th ed. St. Paul, MN: West Group.

Getches, David H., Charles F. Wilkinson, and Robert A. Williams Jr. 2005. *Federal Indian Law.* 5th ed. St. Paul, MN: West Publishing Co.

Goldberg-Ambrose, Carole. 1995. "Retrocession versus Concurrent Jurisdiction." Paper presented to the Southern California Tribal Chairmen's Association Meeting on Developing Comprehensive Tribal Justice Systems. February.

———. 1997. *Planting Tail Feathers: Tribal Survival and Public Law 280.* Los Angeles: University of California, American Indian Studies Center.

Goldsmith, Andrew, ed. 1991. *Complaints against the Police: The Trend to External Review.* Oxford: Clarendon Press.

Greenfeld, Lawrence A., and Steven K. Smith. 1999. *American Indians and Crime.* NCJ 173386. Washington, DC: U.S. Department of Justice, Office of Justice Programs, Bureau of Justice Statistics. February.

Haarr, R. N. 1997. "Patterns of Interaction in a Police Patrol Bureau: Race and Gender Barriers to Integration." *Justice Quarterly* 14 (1): 53–85.

Hagan, William T. 1980. *Indian Police and Judges: Experiments in Acculturation and Control.* Lincoln: University of Nebraska Press.

Harring, Sidney L. 1982. "Native American Crime in the United States." In *Indians and Criminal Justice*, ed. Laurence French, 93–108. Totowa, NJ: Allan-Weld, Osman and Co.

Johnson, Kevin. 2000. "Tribal Police Isolated in Darkness, Distance." *USA Today*, March 22.

Jones, Oakah L. 1966. "The Origins of the Navajo Indian Police, 1872–1873." *Arizona and the West* 8: 225–38.

Kobetz, R., and C. Hamm. 1970. "Contemporary Problems in Law Enforcement on American Indian Reservations." *Police Chief* 37 (July): 58–61.

Koehler, Marc. 1989. *When Things Go Wrong: Disciplinary Policies for Tribal Departments*. Cambridge, MA: Harvard Project on American Indian Economic Development. May.

Kress, June. 1996. "Office of Community Oriented Policing Services." Paper presented at the 1996 Annual Tribal Criminal Law Update Symposium.

Luna, Eileen M. 1997. "Community Policing in Indian Country." *Church and Society Magazine* (Presbyterian Church [USA]) (March–April): 94–100.

———. 1998. "The Growth and Development of Tribal Police." *Journal of Contemporary Criminal Justice* 14 (1): 75–86.

———. 1999. "Law Enforcement Oversight in the American Indian Community." *Georgetown Public Policy Review* 4 (2): 149–64.

Luna, Eileen, and Samuel Walker. 1997. *A Report on the Oversight Mechanisms of the Albuquerque Police Department*. Albuquerque: City Council.

Luna-Firebaugh, Eileen. 2005. "Violence against Indian Women and the STOP VAIW Program." *Violence against Women: An International and Interdisciplinary Journal* 11 (7): 1–22.

Maniaci, Jim. 2005. "Wauneka Takes a Step Up." *Gallup (NM) Independent*, June 1.

Martin, M. D., and J. Alese. 1995. *A Facility Review and Preliminary Assessment of Detention Needs for the Tohono O'odham Nation*. BIA #95-J4002. Washington, DC: National Institute of Corrections, U.S. Department of Justice, Bureau of Indian Affairs, U.S. Department of Interior Technical Assistance. February.

Martin, S. E. 1992. "The Changing Status of Women Officers: Gender and Power in Police Work." In *The Changing Role of Women in the Criminal Justice System*, ed. I. L. Moyer, 281–305. Prospect Heights, IL: Waveland.

———. 1994. "Outsider within the Station House: The Impact of Race and Gender on Black Women Police." *Social Problems* 41 (3): 383–400.

National Tribal Trial College. 2005. *Domestic Violence in Indian Country: Building a Successful Criminal Case*. Office on Violence against Women, U.S. Department of Justice and Southwest Center for Law and Policy.

Office of the City Auditor, Portland, OR. 1993. *Portland's System for Handling Citizen Complaints about Police Misconduct Can Be Improved*. Report by the Audit Services Division of the City of Portland, Oregon. Report no. 178. January.

Perez, Douglas. 1994. *Common Sense about Police Review*. Philadelphia: Temple University Press.

Perry, Stephen. 2004. *American Indians and Crime*. Washington, DC: U.S. Bureau of Justice Statistics.

Reno, Janet. 1995. "U.S. Department of Justice Commitment to American Indian Tribal Justice Systems." *Judicature* 70, no. 7, 114.

Rolo, Mark Anthony. 2000. "Tribal Cops at Risk Each and Every Day." *Indian Country Today*, December 29.

Ross, Jeffrey Ian, and Larry Gould. 2006. *Native Americans and the Criminal Justice System: Theoretical and Policy Directions*. Boulder, CO: Paradigm Publishers.

San Diego County Citizens Law Enforcement Review Board. 1994. *Annual Report*. San Diego, CA.

Shirley, Joe, Jr. 2005a. "Executive Branch Budget Message to the 20th Navajo Nation Council Budget Session." *Navajo Nation News Page*, September 8.

———. 2005b. "Navajo Nation President Joe Shirley, Jr., Presents Executive Branch Budget to Navajo Nation Council." Press Release, September 8. Accessed at http://www.navajo.org/septnews.htm.

Sowers, Carol. 1998. "Fort McDowell Police Force Is Wracked with Problems." *Arizona Republic*, April 18.

Strickland, Rennard. 1975. *Fire and the Spirits: Cherokee Law from Clan to Court*. Norman: University of Oklahoma Press.

Tate, Michael L. 1977. "John P. Clum and the Origins of an Apache Constabulary, 1874–1877." *American Indian Quarterly* 3:99–120.

Turner, S. 1996. Review of *Breaking and Entering*. In *Wisconsin Women's Law Journal* 11:175.

U.S. Bureau of Indian Affairs (BIA). 1975. *Indian Law Enforcement History*. Washington, DC: BIA.

———. 1995. "Listing of Reservations Where Major Crimes Act Applies by Area Office and Type of Law Enforcement Program." Draft. March 31.

U.S. Commission on Civil Rights, Office of Civil Rights Evaluation. 2003. *A Quiet Crisis*. Washington, DC: U.S. Commission on Civil Rights.

U.S. Department of the Interior, Office of Inspector General. 2004. *Neither Safe nor Secure: An Assessment of Indian Detention Facilities*. Report no. 2004-I-0056. September.

Wagner, Dennis. 1997. "Tribal Officer Accused of Taking Files: Reports Dealt with Indian Gangs." *Arizona Republic,* April 16.

Wakeling, Stewart, et al. 2000. *Policing on American Indian Reservations: A Report to the National Institute of Justice*. Washington, DC: U.S. Department of Justice, Office of Justice Programs. July.

Walker, Samuel. 1977. *A Critical History of Police Reform: The Emergence of Professionalism*. Lanham, MD: Lexington Books.

———. 1992. *The Police in America: An Introduction*. 2nd ed. New York: McGraw-Hill.

———. 1998a. *Popular Justice: A History of American Criminal Justice*. 2nd ed. New York: Oxford University Press.

———. 1998b. *Achieving Police Accountability*. Research brief. New York: Center on Crime, Communities and Culture. September.

———. 1998c. *Citizen Review of the Police: 1998 Update*. Omaha: University of Nebraska.

———. 1999. *The Rights Revolution: Rights and Community in Modern America*. New York: Oxford University Press.

Walker, S., C. Spohn, and M. DeLone. 1996. *The Color of Justice: Race, Ethnicity, and Crime in America*. Belmont, CA: Wadsworth.

Walker, Samuel, and Betsy Wright. 1995. *Citizen Review of the Police, 1994: A National Survey*. Washington, DC: Police Executive Research Forum.

Walker, Samuel, and Betsy Wright Kreisel. 1996. "Varieties of Citizen Review." *American Journal of Police* 15 (3): 65–88.

Walsh, Jim. 1998. "Downward Spiral for Ex–Top Cop: He's Arrested in Marital Fight." *Arizona Republic*, July 22.

INDEX

tribal governments, 11, 27, 30, 65; funding from, 15–16; and jails, 103–4; jurisdiction of, 36–38; police departments of, 25–26; sovereignty of, 34–35; and United States, 9–10
Tribal Self-Government program, 12
turnover rate, 60–61, 62

U.S. Border Patrol, 110
U.S. Bureau of Indian Affairs (BIA), 7, 15, 19, 25, 27, 48(table), 109, 118, 120; certification requirements, 62, 63; Courts of Indian Offenses, 28–29; detention facilities, 103–4, 105; and police budgets, 51–52
U.S. Bureau of Indian Affairs Law Enforcement Services (BIA-LES), 5, 11, 21, 48, 49, 68, 85; funding, 12, 74; lack of accountability of, 51–52; operations of, 49–50
U.S. Congress, 30, 31, 33
U.S. Constitution, 8, 9, 104–5
U.S. Department of Justice, 15, 71, 104, 109, 120
U.S. Supreme Court, 8, 10, 30–32, 34, 37–38, 42, 46

U.S. v. Antelope, 30–31
U.S. v. Clapox, 30
U.S. v. Lara, 32, 37–38
U.S. v. McBratney, 31
U.S. v. Wheeler, 31–32
Utah, 115

Victims of Crime Office, 15, 71
violence, 102; domestic, 65, 67, 69–72, rates of, 12–13, 92
Violence against Women Office, 15

Washington (state), 109; and PL 280, 115, 124; women in law enforcement in, 84, 86–87
Wauneka, Ronni, 85
Whatcom County (Wash.), 109, 112
White Mountain Apache Tribe, 82
Williams v. Lee, 38
Wisconsin, 25; and PL 280, 115, 121–22, 124, 136n14
women: as crime victims, 13, 65, 92; in law enforcement, 66, 83–89, 111, 128

youth, 5, 13, 14, 107, 111, 112

ABOUT THE AUTHOR

Eileen Luna-Firebaugh is an attorney and an associate professor of American Indian Law and Policy at the University of Arizona. She is Choctaw and Cherokee and a member of the Paint Clan, who traditionally enforced the laws of the Cherokee Nation. Descended from judges, Lighthorsemen, and those who held medicine, she is an associate justice of the Colorado River Indian Tribal Appellate Court and a tribal judge for the Sac River Band of the Chickamauga Cherokee. She writes extensively in the field of American Indian tribal police and tribal policy issues.